The Inner Circle Chronicles

Intuitive Leaders of the New Economy Transforming
Lives and Businesses with Global Consciousness
and Spiritual Teachings

Book 4

Other books from Inner Visions Publishing:

Inner Circle Chronicles—Book 1
12 Intuitive Women Leaders of the New Economy,
Transforming Lives and Businesses with Soul and Spirit

Inner Circle Chronicles—Book 2
Intuitive Women Leaders of the New Economy,
Transforming Lives and Businesses with
Divine Heart and Soul Around the World

Inner Circle Chronicles—Book 3
Intuitive Healers Leading the New Economy
with Integrative Health, Soul, and Spirit

Books by Anne Deidre:

Extreme Intuitive Makeover—
55 Keys to Health, Wealth, and Happiness

Miraculous—
How Spiritual Awakening Cured My Depression,
Inspired My Purpose, and Ignited the Intuitive Powers Within

Forthcoming 2016
Intuition: 6 Basic Instincts to Change your Life

The Inner Circle

Chronicles

Intuitive Leaders of the New Economy Transforming Lives and
Businesses with Global Consciousness and Spiritual Teachings

BOOK 4

Inspired and Edited by
Anne Deidre

Inner Visions Publishing
New Hampshire

Published by Inner Visions Publishing
www.InnerVisionsPublishing.com
in collaboration with HenschelHAUS Publishing, Inc.

ISBN:978-1-59598-512-5
E-ISBN:978-1-59598-513-2
Library of Congress Control Number: 2016959688

Printed in the United States of America

*This book is dedicated to all humankind.
May you recognize the Light within
and the ability to expand consciousness
on the planet through your very existence.
Peace within, Peace without.*

Table of Contents

Introduction—Anne Deidre, Editor 2

Life: It's Perfectly Imperfect for a Reason!
    —Kimberly Anderson 4

Diving Into the Abyss—Sandra V. Castillo....................................... 18

Out of the Darkness and N2 The Light!!
    —R.D. Cogburn 32

My Life, My Obstacles, My Serenity —Desiree Gerretzen.......... 42

Amazing Grace—Becky Henderson, M.Ed...................................... 54

It's All In The Journey—Catherine M. Laub 68

Holding Self Back Because of Limitation, Fear,
    and People-Pleasing —Melissa LeBlanc.................................... 78

There Must Be More—Gillian Manuela 88

Love's Evolving Resonance—Yan Yamamoto Ouadfel 100

My Enlightened Life—Gina M. Pirone.. 114

Raise Your Soul's Vibration and Live in Joy
    —Dana K. Stone.. 128

Afterword—Anne Deidre 139

About Inner Visions Publishing.. 141

The Inner Circle Chronicles

Intuitive Leaders of the New Economy Transforming Lives and
Businesses with Global Consciousness and Spiritual Teachings

BOOK 4

Anne Deidre

Anne Deidre is an International Celebrity Expert on Intuition, Certified Medical Intuitive, Best Selling Author and Publisher, Professional Artist, Speaker and Coach. She has been featured on ABC and NBC TV, on The CW TV Network, HuffPost Live, also a FOX News Radio Contributor, on NPR, CBS Radio, Business Talk Radio, and many print publications such as Examiner.com, Beliefnet and *Aspire* magazine.

Anne's work is channeled from the Divine Energy and Frequency that includes Spirit, Ascended Masters, Archangels, and each soul's Divine Self to shift energetic patterns, catalyze dormant gifts and talents, and ignite the Divine intuitive powers within each person.

Anne's transformational gifts allow her to intuitively shine a light into her clients' energy systems and illuminate their hidden and/or dormant Divine gifts and talents that their soul is here to share. Her unique and powerful gifts allow her to shift energetic patterns, heal trauma, and create new patterns so that they can bring their Divine gifts to the world.

Anne has created Visionary Intuitive Academy with platinum private and group coaching for future thought leaders, spiritual teachers, and professional intuitives. Please visit her website for more information.

Contact Information:

Website: www.annedeidre.com
Email: team@annedeidre.com

Introduction

It is an honor to introduce to you the leaders in consciousness pioneering a new earth in the fourth book of the *Inner Circle Chronicles* series. It has been a privilege to work with each author. Every contributor has many gifts to share with the world. All of the co-authors have taken a difficult situation or challenge in their life and been able to look at the bigger picture and therefore shift their own energy. By shifting their own energy, they have helped shift the world into higher consciousness and elevate humanity in the process.

Whether we are dealing with emotional, mental or physical issues, applying spiritual energy and perspective can transform any area of our lives.

I am grateful for every author in the series who has worked with me. Know that in the Hall of Records and in the realm of Spirit, our words and voices matter.

May you be blessed by the words and Divine energy in this book. Namaste.

Love and Blessings,
Anne Deidre

Kimberly Anderson

Kimberly Anderson is an intuitive life coach, author, certified angel reader, relationship coach and Goddess Within Retreat Leader. After years of failed marriages, feelings of defeat at every level, Kimberly found herself being called to step into her power and embrace her Divine gifts to intuitively work with men, women and youth.

She works to create balance and to empower women, teens and young adults, also working with singles and couples to discover and connect with their twin flame and help them to attain the ultimate joy in their relationships, by empowering them in tantric wisdom and techniques.

Contact Information:

Website: www.KimberlyCAnderson.com

Email: Kimberly@KimberlyCAnderson.com

Life: It's Perfectly Imperfect for a Reason!

By Kimberly Anderson

I've known loneliness, I've known defeat, I've failed and have failed again, I've been lost in my own world and overwhelmed, I have hated myself and others, and I have felt like a prisoner. Therefore, I am able to share understanding, life, accomplishment, love, vitality, courage, and freedom. My name is Kimberly Anderson. I am a mother, friend, sister, daughter, ex-wife, wife, entrepreneur, business woman, author, leader, yoga instructor, relationship coach, goddess mentor and spiritual intuitive teacher and leader....

I am coming from a place of I have been there and done that, I have witnessed that, I know what that feels like, and I remember. The Universe, God has put me on this earth to do many wonderful things such as help and encourage women, children and men to help them find their power and balance their feminine and masculine energies. We are Goddesses/Gods. We are light. We need to remember that and embrace it. Not from an ego standpoint, from a humble and grateful and empowered standpoint. I have learned many lessons in my years on the planet. I find it incredible to sit where I am today, knowing what is going on in my life and all the changes yet to come, while still embarking on the journey of my life, empowerment, encouragement, and enlightenment!

My story is long and detailed, and there are many, many changes that have occurred, lives I've lived and thought processes I have gone through. All of our lives are constantly changing, in one direction or another. We all have these amazing lives that we live, sometimes struggle through and survive. We all have lessons to learn, to teach. It is really true that we are all always students and teachers. We, at the most basic level, teach each other. Here is my story:

I have been married three times; I will refer to them as #1, #2, and #3. I have four children and a whole lot of life lessons under my belt. I have come to understand being absolutely desired and absolutely rejected, all in the same relationship.

The first time I was married, I was 18 years old. Not to the person I should've married. Not to the love of my life, or the man of my dreams. Nope, I married a needy, controlling, abusive man who was 8 years older than me. That cost me what I felt were my dreams, passions, and my life. I remember the day we were getting married. We were getting married in my parents' house. My mom and I were upstairs and I got this feeling in my stomach, like spirit punched me right in the gut. I had had that feeling one other time, 2 years earlier when I was sneaking out of my house, and I got "punched in the gut by spirit," and this voice said I would get caught. I didn't listen; I got caught, big time.

Anyway, I told my mom I didn't think I should get married. She said "don't." I felt guilty that we had people over; that she had made my dress and that I would look like an idiot calling it off. I went through with it, and that night my nightmare began. I can remember him telling me, in his loud, deep, authoritative voice (it still makes my skin crawl to think about) "I am 8 years your senior. You have to obey me." On the days I felt brave enough to talk back, I would tell him that "well that just means you're going to be old and dead before me". We were married for 5 years. And really, in reality, all that means was it took me 5 years to get away from him, because I tried all the time. He would go off to work and I would pack everything and leave. Next thing I would know, I was back, to defeat, helplessness, feeling lost, and like I was in hell. Trying to figure out how my life ended up like this and how it was ever going to get better. Then, he would go to work and I would pack up again and leave…this went on for five years.

He was horribly verbally abusive; I didn't know such awful things could be said about me. Or that anyone could ever say something like that to another person. He was mentally abusive, the manipulation and control were just unbearable. He was physically abusive, but never beat me, he was always careful to not leave any kind of marks. Never wanted the outside world to know the truth of what went on behind closed doors. This marriage reminded me of the movie *Sleeping With the Enemy*, only we didn't have money, and he never wanted to touch me intimately, another thing for him to control.

As I have survived and lived through all that, and have gone to classes and have learned about domestic violence, I can look back and see the cycles. I remember despair and defeat, and I remember the honeymoon stage. I remember dealing with it all. I remember he wouldn't let me eat, even while I was pregnant, because he said I was fat. I remember when I told him I wanted a divorce, and he held me prisoner in our apartment for four days until I proved to him I wasn't going to leave. I remember him driving me near the woods to show me and tell me how he could kill me with his bare hands and bury my body and no one would ever find me, and he wouldn't get caught. I remember thinking I deserved this life because I had a pressured abortion before I met him, and God was punishing me.

Yet, there are a lot of things I do not remember. This, I learned, is called survival mode. My mom will bring up things I don't even remember. She lived a different part of the domestic violence. There is the person who lives in it, and the people who live helpless outside of it. In this relationship, I learned survival. I found I was always asking myself, why is it, if I can't stand him, I hate him, I want to be away from him, that I am always going back??? My aunt once told me "there will come a time, when one day I wake up, and I will truly have had enough, I will leave and never look back." Until then, though, I realized I was living in the cycle of abuse and could not get out.

That day came that my aunt spoke of when, as usual, we were fighting; he was screaming at me, I was walking around our little apartment trying to get away from him, and he just kept following me, screaming. I walked into our bedroom, and he was on one side of the bed, I was on the other. Our two-year-old son walked in the room, climbed on the bed and started jumping on it. Our eight-month-old son was in his crib. So, there he is bouncing on the bed, which is a big no-no, and normally would get him screamed at and spanked by number one. So #1 was screaming at me, and I picked up our son, walked out of the bedroom with #1 following in pursuit screaming at me.

I went into the little kitchen with my two-year-old in my arms and just fell to my knees and cried. #1 went to the front door as I had gone to the kitchen; he was getting ready to leave for work. My little one said to me, "Hold on, Mommy." He walked over to his dad with a little toy in his hands, and as he walked up to him, held his toy out like a gun, and said "bang, bang, bang." I heard his dad kind of laugh, and then he left. My son walked back over to me in the kitchen, wrapped his little arms around me giving me the biggest hug a little guy could muster, and said, "It's ok, Mommy, I shot him for us." That was the day I knew I would leave and never look back.

I met my second husband while I was trying to figure out how to get away from the first. At first, we became friends, being that sounding board for each other. He was at the beginning stages of his divorce. We quickly became attracted to each other and then moved in together. I really enjoyed this newfound relationship. I was being treated like a person, I was being loved on. He let me eat!!! However, it wasn't long-lived. I would say this marriage shocked me because of the way he had come in, and he helped me get away from #1 and then how fast our relationship dissolved.

I don't have enough space to say how up and down this marriage was in detail. However, I will start with right after we moved in, he moved out to chase a job out of state. Three months later, and during my divorce trial to #1, I moved out of state with my two little ones to be with him. I believe he had started seeing someone right after he moved there, so we were "done." Then, he wanted me back. That should've been a red flag! However, I moved out there to be with him.

Within a few months, I was court ordered to move back to where I was, and not move outside of the contiguous counties. This was the first of this ever happening. My attorney couldn't believe it. So I moved back, heartbroken. I was totally depressed. I literally only did anything when my kids were with me. I didn't want to leave my house. Then he decided we were "done" again. We were separated for a few years and then got back together. We bought a house, got married, during which we were in another full-blown trial against #1 and we had also decided to start trying to have a baby. Or at least I thought we were.

Then I found out he was cheating on me. I was absolutely heartbroken. OMG, I just couldn't believe it. I couldn't believe anyone would ever cheat on me...My grandma told me to keep a man happy, all you had to do was "be a maid in the parlor, a chef in the kitchen and a whore in the bedroom". I was great at all of those. Maybe slacked a little on the maid in the parlor, but for the other two, I was awesome! I couldn't believe he was cheating on me. There was no need, I couldn't figure out why he needed to cheat when he had a beautiful, naked woman who always wanted intimacy sleeping next to him every night. Just didn't make sense.

I had two options. First, I could confront him, which he would just lie about anyway. And, he had already been accusing me. And you know what that means. The guilty always accuse the innocent. Or second, I hold my tongue. After all, we were in a huge trial against #1, regarding custody, which I already had, and leaving the state to move to California. I chose to hold my tongue and not say anything until the trial was over. I needed him. I needed him to be that doting husband, loving step-father he was pretending to be. I wanted to leave him then, but I wanted to leave the state more.

We wound up pregnant, we were able to move, and we began life in California. Being pregnant and moving didn't help our marriage. We grew further apart and #2 was just never around. He worked two jobs, and was at the gym all the time. I felt like a single parent. We wound up moving to a different city in California due to him changing jobs, and we bought a house. I remember sitting at the computer, trying to figure out how to leave him. Our marriage sucked, and we both admitted it. I was feeling sick, and still nursing our son. My mom asked me if I was pregnant. Now let me just say, I said a resounding NO. I was nursing, I had been diagnosed with hypothyroidism, and I was not menstruating consistently since I had had our son. Plus, he never wanted to be intimate with me. It was so rare that we were, I couldn't even remember the last time, it had been so long.

Well, sure enough, I was pregnant. I took three cheap pregnancy tests, and all three had a dark second line. I cried for the next three days. I wanted out of that marriage so badly, and I was pregnant. God definitely has a bigger plan! So to move this story along, I started noticing as my pregnancy progressed, that #2 was home very little, less than he already was. He wasn't interested in me or any of the kids or the one growing inside me. I have always said that a woman's intuition is a man's worst enemy. I started getting the feeling he was interested in another woman.

Well, three months after I had my precious baby girl, my intuition was proved correct. He was cheating on me again. That was it. I was ready to pack up my four kids and live in my truck. I couldn't stand him. Still can't! We divorced. Years passed. I wound up needing to get a restraining order against him, as he was getting insanely obsessed with me. He went from being the one I could lean on to my enemy.

We have been divorced eleven years now, and I still have to deal with his shit. He is constantly trying to control me in my own home in how I raise my children, what I do, and where we go. He is still taking me to court and he manipulates the court system and uses it as a means to harass me. I still feel like I can't grow my wings and fly because of him.

Because of this marriage, I learned to see truth even when convincingly being lied to. I learned to completely believe in my intuition because it's always right. I am still learning even when afraid to dig deep and find strength, to lean on friends and family, for the truth will prevail. I am learning that even if he's a bully and controlling and always trying to manipulate every situation that I can't let fear come over me. I have to stand up to him, stand up for myself and the truth will show what he is.

So Mr. #3. He was fun. I had said to myself that I would never marry again unless he was just amazing. Well, he was, at least in the beginning. He made me feel important, adored for the first time. He liked my kids, my family, and showed a real interest in them. He wanted to be with me. It was great! Days turned into weeks, turned into months and into years and next thing I knew, I was in a marriage where, he didn't want to do things as a family anymore, there was once again zero intimacy. Where there was once love and happiness now lived resentment and anger. We grew apart.

When I think about #3, I feel for him. I am sad for him. He is a good person, one of the most talented people I have ever met. If you ever want an "oldies" car built, he is your guy! He is just lost. Nothing is ever good enough for him, and he looks to create perfection and finds imperfection in everything, including me. He said he wasn't attracted to me anymore. I was too fat for him, therefore not attracted to me and never wanted to be intimate with me. I just didn't do it for him. He was constantly making comments about my weight. And for the record, I wasn't fat, not even a little. I wasn't a rail, I never have been, but I wasn't fat, and don't forget the hypothyroidism, which at this point was out of control. He told me in the beginning that he liked the idea of family, but in reality, he didn't. He is a loner of sorts. I was crushed when I realized we were going down a path to our marriage ending. I had decided to love him forever, and we could get through anything, I didn't want to get married, he convinced me that he was the guy to marry! I was heartbroken, truly crushed.

For months, I had been really upset with our relationship, and one day, I finally brought myself to the point where I had to talk to him. We went on a three-hour walk and in this time, I told him all the things that were bothering me. He told me that he couldn't make me happy and there is no point in going on. I was floored. I thought we were going to work on things, not call it quits. He found fault in everything. Me, my children, he couldn't stand that ex #2 wouldn't leave me alone, which caused a lot of issues, just everything. I knew divorce was the right thing, even though it hurt, and how sad it made me. I didn't want to be divorced a third time. I wanted to only get married once, have some kids and the white picket fence. But, that wasn't my path, and I have been on a path of lessons. I don't blame him either. I have to thank him, because he did what I was reluctant to do. Admit we were over.

I know God has a bigger picture in mind. God wants me happy and thriving so that I can be all that I am. In this marriage, I learned self-perseverance. I learned that I had to go deeper within, not allow his issues to be my issues. It forced me to see what I really need and deserve in a relationship. I had to stop compromising my needs and desires.

I have always felt like I was held back. Either I didn't think I had enough knowledge, I didn't have the money, or the man I was with didn't believe in me or wouldn't let me do something. I was resentful for my first marriage, I felt like it robbed me of my twenties. I felt held back by the second one, under constant attack.

However, God has put some wonderful people in my life along the way, and I started to find myself. One day a few years back, I was working on my yoga certification and I was outside practicing (my favorite place to do yoga). I had gone for about an hour and was feeling really inspired and in tune with myself. I sat down and started meditating. I am one of those people who just starts by breathing and then thanking God for basically everything. Just being full of gratitude.

So there I was, sitting in lotus, (sort of) or Indian style, I am breathing conscious, controlled breaths, "Thank you, God, for today, for the sun that shines so bright, I just love the sun. Thank you for the soft breeze blowing against my skin, for the birds that are chirping. Thank you, God, for my children and always keeping them healthy and safe. I thank you, Lord, for my family and for our house, our cars that we can get around. Thank you, Lord, for all the opportunities that you send me and for the experiences, good and bad, and the abuse and pain I have gone through, so that I may help other women struggling."

WAIT! WHAT did I say????? I couldn't believe that came out of my mouth. I had been doing this routine for months, an hour yoga outside, and then meditation. Never had I said that.

In that moment, I was changed. All the regret, resentment and anger I harbored was gone. In that one moment, with that little sentence, my heart was softened. It made perfect sense. Yes, I could help people, but had I not gone through what I had gone though and experienced what I had, I could not get on the same level and help like I can. I couldn't connect on the same level as someone had I not gone through that stuff.

I sat there, shocked at what had come out of my mouth. Tears came down my face, "Thank you, God, thank you, God, thank you, God. You are so mighty and wise"! I knew I was here on this earth to help women, help women find their inner goddess, their strength. I know I am here to help all people to find their true selves. I am so grateful for the opportunities that come my way, for the opportunities to help me move into the person I am meant to be. I am grateful.

Remember, I said God has a plan? Well, I am also a realtor, and one day, I was meeting a new client and lo and behold, I met my beloved, my soulmate, my twin flame, the love of my life. God is so good! We are building an incredible life together with all of our children and loving every minute of it!

I am the perfect person to say true love doesn't exist. But it does, it's powerful, it's exciting, it's silly, it's fun and it is real!

I have always been intuitive, and I've known it. My kids are, too. I can look back on my life and see where I knew something was going to happen, or where I knew the answer, or when I have manifested something in my life. I am so grateful. I am now using that gift with my research and further certifications and have created a beautiful intuitive business. I coach women, men, couples, and youth. I offer one-on-one sessions, group sessions and teleconferences. I hold day and weekend seminars. I offer goddess seminars both day and weekends. I offer intuitive readings, both in group and one on one. My business is always growing as spirit leads me. Please visit my website, www.KimberlyCAnderson.com, and see where and how I may help you.

Love and Light,
Kimberly

Here are some of my upcoming events.
For more information, please visit www.KimberlyCAnderson.com

Beloved: I work with my intuitive gifts bringing together the twin flame tantric retreat where I work with Gods and Goddesses facilitating the twin flame energy, whether you come with your twin flame or you come with your partner and you are looking to bring in your twin flame. This powerful retreat will teach you how to honor yourself, your partner and to pull in twin flame energy using tantric secrets, energy and intention.
Prerequisite: **Meet Me in Love retreat**.

Inspiring the Goddess Within: Goddess tele-class, special 2-hour event. I will deliver Goddess messages to each person, man or woman, helping to dissolve any blocks, giving you guidance to bring the

Goddess within you to the surface and balance your Divine Femi-nine and masculine energies. This tele-class is for you. Hear from the Goddess to help you on your path.

G3: Goddess to the 3rd Power! (Women only) In this day-long seminar, we will have discussions and breakout groups to learn to feel and harness your goddess power, hear your voice, learn your yes/your no. Self-image (love yourself), energy work, flower power, learn how at every stage of our lives as girls and women we can al-ways pull from our inner power of the Maiden, Mother and Crone. Seminar open to 14-year-olds and up. So bring your mothers, aunts, sisters, nieces and daughters.

Divine Feminine Goddess weekend: (Women only) In this sem-inar, we will come together as sister Goddesses. We will empower each other through our Shakti, learn from each other. I will give Goddess readings, you will learn about flower power on a deeper level, learning your Yes/No, meditation and self-love. Learn about the female orgasm. Chakra energy healing. This weekend is open to 18-year-olds and above. Space is Limited

Meet Me in Love Couples weekend seminar: In this weekend, we learn about the female and male orgasm, how to have longer and deeper orgasms. Learn about our bodies, how together we can enrich each other. It's not just sex, it's lovemaking and making love, it is powerful, and it is the highest form of meditation. We will dis-cuss honoring the beloved. How to keep the ritual of your love sa-cred. We will learn different modalities of touch, kiss and loving each other up, tantric secrets, energy, plus a whole lot more.

Growing into Consciousness: This age-appropriate workshop is for the youth. Growing into consciousness, understanding your self-worth, your body, energy, intention, relationships and how we im-pact one another. This inspiring workshop helps to identify who you really are, your desires and how to grow to magnificence. This workshop helps teens to be better educated about relationships, giving them an advantage their parents didn't get; and offers sup-port to talk about the "stuff" they need to talk about. Getting to the true "grit" of what all of this means and understanding what a great relationship looks like so you don't find yourself in a bad relationship or a domestic violence situation. This is your sex-ed class they should have taught in school. Ages 14-19 years old.

Relationship Repair: So somewhere along the line you realized that you are feeling/falling out of love. The desire is gone, the passion for each other has turned into passion for other things. Your desire for each other has dwindled and intimacy has suffered.

In this 6-month program, you will rekindle your love for each other, fire up the desire and return to your love state. This program is for those who wish to fix what is broken and become the couple they once were and want to be again. This is also for those who are on the verge of divorce and want to put in that last ditch effort to bring the relationship back. This course is cheaper than divorce and beats the heartache that goes with it. Allow me to teach you about each other and offer new and creative ways to honor each other and fall in love all over again. This will not work for all couples; however, it is worth it if you can come together again and live happily ever after, and it's still worth it if you don't.

This program teaches you how to love and honor yourself, your partner, and you can carry it into your next relationship. In this course, you will receive a couple's spiritual numerology reading. Learning about who you and your partner truly are and what makes them tick. You will learn basic tantric techniques to practice with each other bringing your intimacy to a whole new level. Learning how to love and honor each other and so much more. This program requires a commitment and has homework and home practice, giving you tools and techniques to use throughout your renewed relationship!

Sandra V. Castillo

*S*andra V. Castillo is an author, empath and spiritual intuitive. A retired licensed massage therapist, it was during her work as a therapist that she saw the connection of how our body's health is directly related to our state of mind and our emotions affecting not only the relationship we have with ourselves and with our loved ones, but also the purpose we believe we were meant to live.

It was her own failing health where she came to understand how certain beliefs about ourselves that were created in childhood can become lies that we silently tell ourselves that end up shaping our lives in mind, body and spirit. It wasn't until she met Anne Deidre and through the process of writing her chapter for this book did she find, through Anne's support and guidance, the strength in her own intuitive abilities for her own healing transformation.

Since she has written her chapter, Sandra has found a deeper connection to God. She has had a mystical reawakening and is passionate about assisting others remembering the truth of who they are. She works as a transformational catalyst helping others work holistically with mind, body and spirit through relationships. Having a deep belief in holistic health, Sandra is currently pursuing her bachelor's degree in Psychology and is eager to combine other healing modalities such as reiki, medical intuitive and spiritual counseling.

Special thank you to my family for their love and patience. I would also like to give a big thank you to Anne Deidre, Jane Lorenz, David Essel M.S., Claire Zammit Ph. D.C., and Katherine Woodward Thomas MA, MFT of Feminine Power Mastery for their support and guidance through my journey. I love you all!

Contact Information:
Website: www.infinitetruthseeker.com
E-Mail: truthseeker5731@gmail.com

Diving Into the Abyss

HOW DEPRESSION BECAME MY PATH TO MY TRUE SELF

By Sandra V. Castillo

You can say I was born aware. Life looked absolutely beautiful to me and it was full of exciting adventures as I interacted with both spiritual and earthly realms simultaneously. As I was growing up, little by little, I learned that no one else around me could see what I was seeing nor did they believe the truth that our spiritual realm co-exists with us.

Because as humans, we are taught how to live a life of survival, I soon became confused and angry by the limitations enforced upon me that blocked that spiritual world from me. As the beautiful and adventurous experiences started to change into dark, negative, and painful events, I became emotionally scarred and branded as weird and crazy.

By the time I was five years old, I didn't want anything to do with my purpose here on earth and totally rejected God, my psychic and spiritual gifts, and the spiritual realm I knew to exist. This left me feeling completely abandoned, unworthy, undeserving and unloved.

Since the age of five, my life has been riddled with spiritual, mystical, and paranormal experiences, coupled with overwhelmingly heavy emotions, thoughts of suicide, and physical health issues doctors could not diagnose. I also had an extremely difficult time in school, as I seemed to have been born with the inability to focus, concentrate, memorize and comprehend. Although I loved to learn and I was eager to do well and despite professional help, I had a tremendous time trying to figure out how to study. All this, of course, had an impact on relationships with my friends and family. Slowly I became less social because I always felt awkward, odd, and different, which made it hard for me to relate and keep friends.

Life has taken its toll on me mentally, emotionally, and physically. I had been living my whole life feeling like I had to figure out, by myself, how to survive on my own and without anyone being able to help me. Living my life this way, with the constant pressure I put on myself to keep my secret hidden, brought so much stress to my body, mind, and spirit that I finally realized I had to change and accept the fact that the path I have been on attracted more pain and suffering, more than what I could even bear.

It was 2006, a few weeks before my wedding. My level of anxiety was at an all-time high. Coupled by my depleting energy, painful body, and deep depression, I was worried that if I didn't take the chance and risk changing my ways, right now, I'll never get another opportunity to live life like I was meant to.

For the first time since I was ten years old, I reached out to Spirit and asked Jesus for some help, guidance, and understanding. Asking Jesus to put me on my path that he knows is right for me because I had lost my way and have no idea which way to go.

About one month later, a week after our honeymoon, I had the craziest and most amazing mystical experience. On our way home from working out, Jesus's face appeared in an immense bright white light at the dead end of our street. I was in awe of what I was experiencing, but also knew that I was crazy because my husband didn't see it. I accepted the experience wholeheartedly, fully expecting my life to be healed. I was so excited, I could not wait to see what that would look like.

The next morning, when I got up from my bed, I passed out. When I woke up again, I was confused. What the hell just happened? This was NOT what I had in mind for a healing. I got the exact opposite!

After a few months of seeing doctors, I found out that my endocrine system was completely shot; my kidneys, adrenals, and thyroid were completely fatigued. Doctors could not understand why I was not improving and my blood work did not show any signs as to why. What ensued after this incident was more of what I had experienced in my life, but exponentially intensified.

Eventually, I was told that I have acute chronic fatigue syndrome with a mild case of fibromyalgia. My health never recovered. I had to close my massage business, my husband lost his job, and we lost our home to foreclosure, having to rely on both our families for financial help. That was our marriage.

It took me nearly six years since then to finally figure out that what I had to change wasn't in how I was trying to heal my physical body, but how I feel and believe in myself. Making this choice had the largest impact on my marriage and my life. Everything fell apart in our relationship. I was hiding psychic experiences from my husband because it seemed to really make him uncomfortable. I was tired of hiding in my own home and felt trapped.

After some time, seeing the stark differences between my husband and myself, I knew that a divorce was the right decision. As the process of the divorce was nearing its end, I moved out into my own place. Within a week of living on my own, I was so surprised that some of the fatigue had lifted. The lightness I felt in my body was also proof that I was headed in the right direction.

Feeling like I had more space in my mind and heart, my next challenge surfaced into that space: my deep-seated anger and hatred for God. This was big and I needed help. I knew that I needed to be open to whoever could help me.

I had joined an eight-week group program with Anne Deidre, and on one particular call, Anne performed an energy clearing and energy channeling on me that had a profound effect on my aura and heart chakra. That night, as I was lying in bed, I could feel two balls of energy hovering in front of me over my heart chakra. They began to merge, became one, and slowly dropped into my chest. What those two balls of energy were, I cannot tell you. All I know is that I felt warmth spreading into my chest, feeling peaceful and whole-hearted.

After the eight-week course, I was disappointed to find myself undergoing another bout of depression. In the past, I had learned to submerge whatever fear that came up in my heart and mind. Today, I decided to let myself go and allow the fear to rise up from the depth of my depression. Instead of retreating from it, I thought, *What would happen if I dove into it? I can see it's dark in there. So, what if I went in to take a look?*

I took the dive in. I imagined it like taking a dive into the abyss. I let the darkness of the fear envelop me. To my surprise, I started to cry and a wave of sadness came right over me. *This is my fear?* I gradually realized that fear was covering up a deep sadness. *How long have I had this?* I wondered, traveling back in my memory to when I was a five-year-old. I was honestly shocked to see myself yelling at God, telling him how much I hated him for putting me down here with no one to help me.

God had given me my gifts with no way of learning how to use them. I can hear myself denouncing God; I rejected my gifts and vowed to never be a part of them. I remember the feeling that I had to figure things out for myself by myself. I felt heartbroken, un-loved, undeserving, unworthy, lonely and lost.

This is why I am depressed? It dawned on me that by rejecting God, I had inadvertently rejected myself. I had no self-acceptance. I believed that I deserved the pain and suffering. That's exactly how my life played out. Once I became conscious of this, it seemed like all the pain and suffering from my life flooded into my inner being. I took it all in, and it felt like I was drowning.

The darkness of the depression surrounded me as if I drifted down into the abyss. The sobbing came and went until I felt like I purged all emotions and thoughts. What I did next came naturally to me. I called out to God.

God! Please help me!

You know I truly do love you.

I'm sorry I said I don't need you.

I'm sorry that I said that I don't believe in you because you know that I do and I always will.

Please forgive me.

Take my soul, take me as I am. Mold this life as you have always had intended and make it as astounding and wonderful as you are.

I beg you to help me, because I do not know what is real and what is not real.

I am terrified of my own life because I have lived it as though I do not exist and it has become too painful for me to bear anymore.

Take it, my soul, and do what you want with it because I am forever yours.

Thank you.

The next day, I woke up feeling like I had a hangover. I decided to be gentle with myself as if I had the flu, taking care with what I thought I needed and allowing myself to go through the process of healing, cleansing and resting.

As I was reading my emails, I saw a title to a blog: *"Are you an empath?"* I didn't know much about it, but for some reason the subject really piqued my interest. It went on to describe that people who are not aware they are empaths don't know they can pick up on other people's emotions and can suffer from depression and an overwhelming sense of heaviness.

Can this be true? Am I an empath?

There was a sense of opening stillness and silence that brushed a smile on my face. In an instant, I knew the answer. I am an empath.

The house I was living in had been foreclosed on. The divorce was finalized and I saw the opportunity to continue to do deeper personal work with feminine power mastery course and to develop and strengthen my intuitive gifts with Anne. I was still acutely fatigued with bouts of depression and anxiety that were running my life. So I decided to move in with my parents to reduce the stress of having to pay bills and use that money towards rebuilding my physical, mental, emotional, and intuitive foundation. By the end of that journey, I hoped I could start living a more productive life.

At first, I was excited to move in and start my journey. I didn't feel as isolated being closer to my family. I did feel more energized and this energy gave me some confidence in being able to accomplish what I had set out to do. It did appear that way at first, but as time moved on and I started to work with Anne and the mastery course, I was slowly falling behind and had a hard time concentrating. Once again, things were becoming heavy and difficult to handle.

In spite of the increasing heaviness, I was having wonderful spiritual breakthroughs. However, when I sat down to do my journaling, I couldn't remember the experience, and my mind would go blank. I tried forcing myself to write something, but what came out was a series of questions: *Why can't I hear you? Why can't I understand? I feel so confused. Why can't I see you? Even though I know you are there, I feel like I don't even know you anymore.*

At the same time, living with my parents proved to be more difficult than I had anticipated. Seeing my sedentary state only made my parents nervous for me. All I wanted was to sleep and rest. Instead, I had to look busy and active so that they could relax.

When practicing to see how my intuitive gifts were working, my relationship with my mother became strained. It did take some time for me to see the connection but it came to my knowledge how strong of a connection I have with my mother, empathically. When my mother suffered Bell's palsy, I apparently suffered pain and discomfort as my mother did. *This is great, now I know how my empathic ability works.* But it took me some time to see this, because my own body hurt all the time and I attributed the pain to be my own issue. What also complicated the experience was the fact that my emotional confusion was so convoluted that I couldn't pull apart my own emotions with those of my mother.

When summer came and my parents went up north, I had the place to myself. It was wonderful! It was time for some much-needed rest and relaxation. It wasn't until then that I noticed how stressed out I was. Working with Anne, coupled with doing the mastery course and living with my parents, was a lot for me to handle, especially for someone who had been living like a vegetable for the past nine years. But I was determined to stick with it. For some reason I felt like I had to.

Having the house to myself meant I could rest with no pressure around me. I could feel myself expand. One day, as I was sitting outside taking in nature, a question came to my mind: *Ask for a miracle?*

Yeah right! I thought suspiciously. I felt like I was being tricked. "Ok, I want my body to be healed." With that, I let it go. No way was I expecting for that ever to happen. With everything I've been through so far, I'm still too fatigued to work, play, or live any kind of a normal life.

I vacillated between spiritual breakthroughs and total mental fogginess. Confused as to why these downloads of knowledge left as quickly as they came, I started to doubt the work I was doing. I couldn't process anything. This was becoming exceedingly frustrating and disappointing. I just stopped trying to understand anymore.

Despite what Anne was trying to help me do and despite what tools I received from the mastery course, I felt completely lost. Perhaps I had veered onto the wrong path. I was losing faith in my intuitive abilities and my hope of a normal life. I wanted to run away and started to worry about my financial situation because I was still not able to work. *Am I in a state of illusion? Did I ask for something that isn't realistic to my life?* I imagined myself in a boat floating on top of the black abyss with nothing but thick, gray fog all around me, sitting completely still, going nowhere.

When my parents returned, it was obvious that the relationship with my father was the next one to become strained. I felt angry, anxious, frustrated, and irritated. I suffered insomnia for a few weeks followed by intense migraines for a month. By the New Year, the stress on my body took its toll. I was not coping well at all. My fears and anxiety was at an all-time high. My kidneys were hurting and throbbing and my urine had changed color. I was very concerned and scared.

At the time, there was no indication anything was going on with my parents. This was a good time to ask Spirit if there were any issues related to how I was feeling, and to please let me know.

The moment I began to consider seeing a urologist, my mother told me that my father hadn't been feeling well and his doctor had him get an MRI to rule out any kidney issues. He was at his doctor's office getting the results as my mother and I were speaking. Whoa! The second I heard this, the pain in my back dissipated.

I was shocked and pleasantly surprised. A newfound sense of confidence in my empathic abilities rushed into my heart. I was so relieved I was okay. Now that I knew what my father was feeling and going through and how it matched my own feelings, I consciously kept a sense of safety and nurturing in my mind and heart, to also take care and to be gentle with myself.

Thankfully, my father did not have any real threat to his kidneys; the symptoms were secondary to a bacterial infection. As my father's health improved, signs of my own issues became obvious. The reaction my body was undergoing was puzzling, to say the least. My body was acting as if I were going through some major stressful trauma. But I know that I am okay. I've dealt with all of the emotional and relationship issues, past and present. There is no current event that's of any danger to me. So, what is it? There has to be some kind of chemical imbalance, somewhere in my body.

Time for a talk, God. *"You know I have done everything possible I can do on my own. I know I am okay and safe. There is obviously a specific kind of chemical imbalance taking place here. If there is someone who could help me with this exact problem, please bring them into my life. Guide me to them. Whatever the issue is, you know I will do what needs to get done. Thank you."*

Over the past three days, I had gotten three signs from three different people for the same doctor. I did not waste any time to go see the doctor, a gynecologist, who assured me that my issues were most likely due to a hormonal imbalance. I was excited for once; he seemed to act as if he knew that this treatment would help me.

When my blood work came in, I was expecting to hear the same result I had always heard throughout my life. I was wrong! My testosterone level was extremely low; the doctor even considered my levels to be non-existent. He reassured me again that this hormone treatment would give me my life back.

My first treatment was like putting my finger in a socket; absolutely every issue I ever had disappeared. The fatigue, depression, and anxiety were gone. The pain in my body was gone. The walls blocking my focus were gone. No fogginess and my memory seemed to be improving. I'm totally blown away. I am so thankful. I will always be grateful for the rest of my life.

I had gotten my miracle. It may have come in a pill, but I'm not judging. These treatments have given me hope for a future. Hope for a happier and healthier life full of loving friends and hope for a happier romantic relationship. It gave me a sense that life is truly a gift. Standing in the light of this realization melted away any doubt I had of feeling like was undeserving and unloved.

I now have rooted within myself a stronger sense of identity that has fueled my determination to live a more purposeful life. This new sense was unexpected. Although I knew I needed to change but I didn't expect that this change would be felt deeply inside my inner being. Some of the changes were instantaneous, that's why I call it a miracle.

The more immediate changes were physical. Fatigue, achy joints and depression seemed to be replaced by increased energy, painless body showered by happiness, peace and desire. My life seems to have more depth. I love more deeply. I feel more deeply, I have a deeper understanding, I can see deeper into things and people, I feel a deeper connection to the universe and God, a much better understanding of being in oneness with everything and everyone. All was made possible by having a stronger sense of self.

Because of these changes, my relationship at home has improved without anyone needing to change. My perspective of myself has changed. It wasn't in discovering something new about myself that was never there, but unearthing a revelation of who I am. In that way, this experience has already altered my perspective of my empathic abilities. Which I am excited to see what that journey will reveal.

The answer wasn't in searching outside of myself for something I lacked or have someone else give me what I thought was missing. It was going inside and into my own abyss that I simply embraced that part of myself that I had left behind. Who am I? I am that same little girl who knows that our divine realm and our divine family co-exists with us as one. I am an empath. I am a lover. I am a friend. I am deserving. I am worthy and I am a force to be reckoned with.

Today, as a force of energy, I understand that I am that white light underneath that black muck. That black muck was my initial fear that was there to protect me and to keep me safe. It wasn't the darkness of the abyss or the black muck that was dangerous to me and my life, it was holding onto the fear for too long and that fear had hidden itself behind a belief that said I am unloving, I am unworthy. Holding onto that fear for an extended amount of time made me forget what were my real issues and covered who I truly am.

As I stand here today as a witness to my own healing, I can look back at my life with different eyes. Where I once thought that life was making me suffer through pain, depression, loneliness and isolation changed into seeing where I have learned, in my life journey, that some of our answers to life challenges are meant to be lived into. We are meant to experience our answers because it's how we are empowered with wisdom. That wisdom endowed me with compassion and forgiveness for myself for the choices I made throughout my life. Those seemingly bad and wrong choices, however painful, are gems and treasures to me now because they transformed my life when I was able and ready to let them go. Now I see how life has made me more of value. I value my friends and family. I see the value of what I want to do. I see the value of what I can do. I see the value of having compassion and forgiveness for others who are going through their own transformation by empowering them through their own process.

I am starting my life from scratch and building a new foundation for a new life that will be fortified with integrity, strength and authenticity. My life will now have a new structure that is supported by love, joy, happiness and oneness

We come to know who we are through our challenges, however severe or subtle our circumstances may be, our fears affect us the same. Our challenges are calls for us to evolve. When we ignore them for too long, they build up in negative ways: our bodies with pain and disease, it affects our minds with negative thinking and attitudes, it affects our emotions with anger, hate and sadness, it affects our spirit by sensing ourselves as separate from our spiritual nature, it affects our relationship with intolerance, violence and blocks intimacy from those whom we love.

The answers come when we have the courage to look into our darker sides, into our circumstances that are currently taking place. There is no other way but through. This much I know is true. Embrace your darker side in order to find that treasure. Embracing our darker side is what make us whole, it makes us authentic. It can help us to remain true to ourselves. Being authentic can keep you align to the energy of miracles. However small a miracle is, it is as distinctive and unique to who you are.

By taking on this huge undertaking, we will know ourselves not only by relying on our higher selves, but by illuminating the lies we have accepted as the truth of who we are. Once we are aware of the part of us that we didn't realize is shaping our lives, we can take back our power to create our own life story as we were truly meant to live it.

Ryan D. Cogburn

Ryan Cogburn is an insurance agent and former stockbroker who grew up in the high mountains of Colorado on a cattle ranch. His early childhood difficulties led him to seek a life of recovery from addiction and explore spirituality. For more than thirty years, Ryan has been touching lives and healing the afflicted, teaching that within the soul there is healing.

Ryan is a writer as well. He is very close to family, and friends find that he has a warm sense of humor. Ryan started "N2 The Light" as a way to get out his message of inner healing through a divine connection found within each of us. Ryan does personal mentoring and is the consummate spiritual guide. Ryan is a spiritual sage and a great cook!

Contact information:

Websites: www.mindsetmasterz.com, www.ryancogburn.com

Email: rdcogburn@gmail.com

Tel: 800-820-0607

Out of the Darkness and N2 The Light!!

By Ryan D. Cogburn

A man is at his best when he is being himself. That was what I would learn to live by. Just me! Just Ryan! I wondered what that meant . . . You are reading the story of a man who was transformed by particularly difficult circumstances. You have read stories about how people get down from losing a job or losing a business. Maybe they have lost a loved one or suffered from a debilitating disease. Perhaps they were ruined financially and forced to live on the street.

Whatever the story is, we learn to feel for these poor souls who are down or discouraged. The stories about the veteran who lost a limb or people who lose the use of all their limbs, but through perseverance, fight back and struggle to become more than anyone thought possible. These miracle people are all around. My story is nothing like that except that I did struggle and I did persevere. I even learned to become so much more than anyone thought possible. I am a champion, but that is not what my story is about.

My story is about a man who was once a very lost and lonely boy. At first, he had it all, but then things became difficult. He was loved by a happy mother and father who were deeply in love and committed to each other. Perhaps the good start had a reason, but what followed was devastating.

Around age eight, the boy witnessed his parents' divorce. School became very difficult for him. The fights his mom and dad had late at night kept him up and he worried intensely about how to fix it all.

Why did he think it was his problem? I don't know. Kids just do!

Soon his grades began to fail as he spaced out at school. He got yelled at for poor grades. The yelling made him withdraw. He had scary dreams at night, but never talked about them. He became overweight and was known as the fat, freckled kid. He had a heart condition and asthma and was forced to sit out of PE, which he absolutely loved. He loved competing. His teachers put him down. He fought with his brothers.

Soon his parents were divorced and his mother died from cancer when the boy was 13. He ran away from home and began experimenting with drugs. People started to call him "Stony." His already damaged self-esteem became non-existent.

Soon his parents moved him to their ranch, where he learned to work. He loved hard work and the "attaboys" that went with it. He learned that he could ride horses and became a rodeo cowboy, winning trophies and getting pats on the back at school.

Sure, there were the doubters, but the people who liked him more than made up for the doubt. He was beginning to have some self-esteem, but things at home were tough. Mom had died and working alone and riding his horse or motorbike for hours were his way of escape. He hunted by himself or with a friend or brother. Fishing was always a highlight, too.

Life was pretty good again, but trouble wasn't far away. One day, he skipped school because of the enticement of having some extra cash by working at the local feed store unloading a truck. Most kids don't skip school to go work their guts out, but if you're offered $50, you'll do about anything when you're a teenager.

Well, the day ended on a very sour note when suddenly that boy felt a rope around his neck as he was leaving the feed store. Some kids were having fun, but took it too far. The rope around his neck was thrown over the rafters and he was hung by his neck. The life left his body as he fainted. The boys left him for dead as he lay on the wooden floor unconscious. They ran away.

Someone woke him by shaking him, only to let him know that his dad was there. He never talked about that day, but needless to say, whatever self-esteem he had, it was certainly gone. He would wonder why he was so bad that he deserved to die. Why couldn't he be popular or liked?

Soon he started to make new friends and discovered that pot was a great escape and so much fun. He found this magic the year he graduated. He had been told he could leave home as soon as he finished high school, so he did. As it turned out, life was hard and he was not prepared.

Drug addiction became the theme of his life and he soon found that drinking was his favorite medication. Getting blitzed was the best escape he could find. His life continued to have failure after failure. No self-esteem was to be found.

Addiction was a hard life and money was in short supply as it was not much more than a contribution to the cause. Failed marriages and poor self-image would undo his every attempt to make something of his life.

* * * * *

* * * * *

J wrote this narrative in third person because I remotely remember what it was like to be in those circumstances. I also want you, the reader, to see me from the perspective of a person on the outside, because now I will take you inside to show you what radical transformation looks like!!

For me, it's about that perseverance and a will to survive. Then finding something so amazing and bigger than life. Like a giant secret that's so big no one sees it!

That secret is me. I am Ryan and I'm a healer!

You see, there is so much more to my story than I can tell here or even in an entire book. Yes, it would probably make a great movie if I ever get around to writing it. Forget all that because my message to my reader is that radical transformation can and will happen to you in your life.

For some reason, I was blessed with the ability to understand the inner workings of the soul. I submit to you that all we do on this earth is "Soul Work."

My "Soul Work" started when I was very young. It was in my dreams. I was horrified of falling and drowning. I overcame those things in my dreams but not without a cost. Remember that boy who was so troubled at school? Well, I was so horrified of my dreams that I still peed my pants in school clear up to the fourth grade. No one knew that the reason was this "Soul Work" happening to me at night.

In third grade, I taught my teacher a faster way to subtract. I was able to do subtraction three or four times faster than the other kids and even my teacher and it was always 100% correct. When I show it to people today, they are blown away.

I knew something was very different with me very early on. In sixth grade, I was so spaced out I could hardly function due to my parents' problems so my teacher banned me to the school cafeteria to wash dishes. One day, I showed one of the ladies in the cafeteria my math trick, so they tested my IQ. They accused me of cheating somehow because I aced their test.

Now please understand that I was the kid who was spaced out in class and got in a fight on the playground about every other day. Not exactly the child who was obedient and liked to study. Even then, I knew it was just my intuition taking over. I had a belief that when I went away, there was a magical power inside me.

I learned to hide from people mostly. I passed my classes with little effort but never did well. I had an intense interest in what people were really like when no one was around. I became fairly likable and knew that fighting was not good. I had been warned not to fight many times. I finally got to a point where I would refuse to fight.

Then my teen years and all the time alone out in the country helped me to realize that I could really soar from the inside. Whether it was on a horse or a motorcycle or a tractor or anything else, I knew I was of some value for reasons no one knew about.

Let me skip forward to my recovery from drug and alcohol addiction. I was divorced at age 22 when I first tried to sober up. Having one year of sobriety was amazing. People were proud of me and I was happy like I had never been before. I did it all to save my marriage but when it didn't work, I found myself drinking more than ever. I lasted another four years. The end would be rough for me.

Soon, I found myself living in the most expensive place on earth with no money, no job, no friends, and no self-esteem—homeless and helpless. I went to my good friend, who was my pastor. He simply told me I needed to be removed from society and was unable to function for a number of reasons.

From there, I spent thirty days in a treatment facility, which changed my life dramatically. All the players were there at the right time with the right words and right actions for me. It was as if God himself had personally arranged all that for me.

Today, I have almost thirty years of sobriety. Yes, that is cool, but sobriety was never enough. What I have to tell you now is the good stuff!

What sobriety gave me was hope. It gave me back myself and it gave me structure. It set me on a path of Spiritual growth. So many of the things from the "BIG BOOK" of AA have been my marching orders. Certain phrases and sentences seem to ring out and ring true in every facet of my life. The human condition has never been described more accurately as it is in that book.

For me, I had to use what I knew to stay sober. I had to be thorough and completely honest with myself. I was accused of being schizoid, amongst other things, so I wanted all the information I could find.

What I learned transformed me. Today, I have been the top salesman at every job I have had and I am in business for myself. Life has had its ups and downs, but I recover because no matter how difficult my circumstances become, I have a process. When I am down and out and need help, I can connect to my higher power and my friends and family.

The process I have learned and developed came from taking the very best things I have learned from Christianity, AA, and self-help gurus like Tony Robbins, Zig Ziglar, and Jim Rohn.

My first sales mentor was Tom Hopkins, renowned trainer and speaker, as well as author of *How to Master the Art of Selling.* I read like a hungry soul and devour information at a high rate simply because the blessing of learning is such an important and integral part of my life.

My intuition has always served me well. I learned in fifth grade that sometimes you just know things. In a calm state, I could come up with amazing results just using what I knew to be true. This led to many other discoveries and breakthroughs. I try to help people have those same breakthroughs within themselves. My system is amazing and I invite you to experience the supernatural elements of your own soul in my "N2 The Light" series.

Sometimes there were breakthroughs or those "white light" moments, but everything was real. Even the out-of-body experience I had was too real.

I struggled. I learned, I suffered, and I overcame. I found that life could be far worse with no medication than I ever imagined. Being trapped in my own hell was at times unbearable. The emotional pain could get a strangle hold on me.

Over time, I learned to take life one day at a time. I learned that I had to be aware of myself and what state of existence I was choosing to be in. I learned that there were some pretty high places I could soar to within my own soul and I learned to walk in the light of the very love that lived within me. I am strong, I am powerful, I am confident. I can become, I can overcome, and I can transform!

Transformation for me has meant staying in the learning mode. Being cocky and arrogant is a set-up! Humility is the way of the wise! Humble, playful, insightful, and irresistible. Those were the character traits I most admired in others and took on for myself.

You see, we cannot see ourselves unless we have a mirror. We see others very well, though. What we have failed to understand is that I am your source and you are mine. Or we could say that the Source of all things is revealed through us from one to another.

The problem begins when we decide to be negative or closed rather than positive and open. Our true identity is found in what we see and experience.

Never think that quietness is mistaken for being closed. If you would dare to sit with me quietly I would show you the great power in receiving from me without speaking. We must quiet ourselves, as we must also express ourselves. Finding our true nature is a task that will require all we can give it! I provided this exercise to make a point about our spiritual walk in this life. We are made of love!

Everything that exists is made of love and love is the very fabric of our molecular existence, right down to the tiniest particles, which we have not yet seen but we know about, called neutrinos.

That is a discussion for later but I wanted to show you that the life you live outside yourself, in other words, the things you see daily, smell daily, hear daily, taste daily and learn and know are also within you. You are a total being created in the image of God. Since the greater one lives within you, then you are certainly irresistible!!

What I work with people on and what I can do are miraculous, although I would tell you that it's you not me who is the miracle. One of the strangest things to me is that all the healing and transformation work I've done over the years has been as if I merely introduced people to the magic within themselves! I take no credit for the transformation of another soul, since I am merely the facilitator. What I do take credit for is being able to show those souls their own pathway back to the light.

I created a series of writings and am now teaching live and one-on-one classes in transformational intuition. What you seek and what you need is within you. Learning to unwrap that great gift can be very challenging! You see, I believe it's such a big gift that we are going to need an entire lifetime to unwrap it.

Growing spiritually only makes sense. We grow physically until a certain age and don't we need to learn to mature properly? We take care of our health and tend to our homes to enjoy nice environments. Why is it then that we don't do the same for our Souls? I will lead you in this critical work of preparing yourself for that transformation.

It's my belief that we live forever lives. Some are only concerned with the here and now. Some will be happy to just have peace and that's admirable, but the truth is that we are so much more! I will guide you to this higher self! I will teach you to heal from the inside. I will teach you to source positive energy, not only into your life, but also into the eternity of others. Yes, this work is not just "worthwhile"—it truly matters!

My program is called "N2 The Light." It starts with a five-step process to move you from your past into your future. Certain Spiritual principles must be observed, but I make everything very simple and understandable. That is my gift. I am able to see and understand the very complex things of not just this life but time and eternity and I can put them into understandable terms.

Of course, there are times when words are just not enough and we must communicate intuitively. You will see more of this as the "light" within humanity increases in a world that is lost and darker than ever. Contrast brings everything into focus in these perilous times. Step "N2 The Light" with me!

Blessings of love and light!!

Desiree Gerretzen

D esiree is an Author, Certified Angel Reader, Akashic Record Reader and Intuitive Healer & Coach. She specializes in Intuitive Relationship Coaching, and works with intuition and energy to help align people with their highest and best life.

Working with Desiree will help provide you with insight and divine wisdom as she clears any false beliefs that do not serve you. She works with Masters, Guides and Angels to help restore the divine blueprint for each client in her readings and coaching programs.

Contact Information:

Website: www.desireepaulamaria.com
Email: desiree@desireepaulamaria.com

My Life, My Obstacles, My Serenity

By Desiree Gerretzen

As soon as you trust yourself you will know how to live.
—Goethe

I was 22 and never felt more alone. I had just received a one-sentence letter from my father stating, "You are an adult, you have your degree, my job is done and you are not welcome back home." I was working as a resident in a hotel in Germany, cleaning rooms and serving meals with some pocket money as a paycheck. How was I going to save some money to find a better job? Where would I find the money to move on? Where do I go? What do I want to do with my life? I was not prepared to step into the world after finishing my studies. I felt insecure, cold, and alone.

I had just received my college degree, came out of a broken relationship and could not find a job so I accepted a job in a hotel in Germany. The hotel was high up in the Alps, and the closest village was 6 km (about 4 miles) away. The hotel organized evenings with live classical music and dances and the guests were mostly elderly people.

As staff for the hotel, the management mostly hired foreign students who wanted to improve their German language skills and people like me who needed some time out. I met lots of wonderful people, we worked together and spent our free time together walking and exploring the area in Bavaria, and in the evenings we chilled out.

At the end of the summer, I wrote my parents a letter that I would love to come home, look for a job and get my life organized. My father replied with his letter and I was shocked. The money I earned was not enough to buy a ticket home and suddenly, it felt like the whole world looked like this big black hole. Was I to stay at the hotel for the rest of my life cleaning rooms? I was devastated and did not see any outcome. Luckily, my aunt and uncle, who was also my father's best friend, came to visit me on their holiday and gave me a ride home.

I grew up in a village in Belgium with my parents and my three brothers. My father was a salesman and was often on the road and my mother stayed home with us. She was strict and well-mannered. When I was twelve, my father became ill and had to stay in bed for a year; my mother had to help him in his business. My father was very strict about money and asking him for money was not easy.

My school education was at a big Catholic school, girls only, and wearing a uniform was obligatory. Going to church was a weekly habit and I loved the stories of Jesus when he performed his miracles and shared his wisdom. The world would look so much better if we treated each other as Jesus did. We did not really talk about our feelings, emotions and doubts. Most of time my parents would whip those off as nonsense.

I joined the Girl Scouts and I loved being outside in nature. I stayed in the Scouts for eleven years and I thoroughly enjoyed the friendships, being outside in nature, going camping, building campfires, and sleeping in tents.

Also at that time, the Flower Power movement came to Europe with influences from India and The Age of Aquarius. This was my first contact with gems and healing tools from Mother Earth. I loved the energy and the new way of thinking.

After returning to Belgium from Germany, my father wanted me to find a job right away. I could start in a fast-food restaurant. My friends from the hotel and I wrote lots of letters to each other and whenever possible, I visited them and welcomed them to visit me as well. It was a time before computers and cellphones where we wrote long letters, putting our feelings, emotions and thoughts on paper in a way not to hurt anyone and on the other hand to make it understandable for the other person. I so enjoyed writing letters and receiving them.

After a year I got another job and moved out of my family home permanently.

My grandfather was a wealthy man and enjoyed having power over the family with his money. When he died, we all inherited some money. Money has been a big issue in the family so when I received the money, I felt like I had to invest it back into the family.

In the late 1950s, two of my father's brothers immigrated to New Zealand and started their families. I heard so many stories about the family in New Zealand and always wanted to visit them. So when I received the inheritance money, I booked my ticket and went to visit them on a five-week trip. Hardly anybody from the family, and it is a big family, had gone to visit them in New Zealand so they were very happy to welcome me and I had a wonderful time. One of my aunts was Maori; she told stories about the trees and birds and the history of their country. It was all so beautiful.

It was such a surprise for me to see that my uncles, even though they had already lived on the other side of the world for twenty years, they had not changed. I had never known them before, but they acted exactly like my father did. They had the same expressions, the same words, the same points of view. They even treated my cousins the same way my father did with us. It felt so familiar and yet so strange. I made a promise to myself that I would do everything in my power to find ME and be ME and not become a product of education. I could embody what a journey this would be.

I got married soon after I returned from New Zealand, moved into our own house, got pregnant and gave birth to our first son. My husband and I both had our careers and I had no problem being a working mum. Our son was not really a happy baby. He refused breastfeeding, got upset when we put him in his little bed, and didn't liked to be touched. We followed lots of advice from "experts" and were so tired.

One day, I put everything aside and followed my intuition and inner knowing. Our son enjoyed the formula milk, was more relaxed, and his stuffed animal became his best friend for many years. We accepted his boundaries and he gained more confidence.

Two years later, our other son arrived and he was so easy. He loved being hugged and was eager to drink and slept like a baby. Everything seemed to be okay. I was happy to take over the business from my mother. She represented a Dutch company specializing in wholesale women's accessories, like scarves and fashion jewelry.

When I took over, we doubled the showroom, received more stock and had to work long hours. My earnings were a percentage of the sales so the more I sold, the higher my income. I loved the job, I loved working with people, I loved trying to match the accessories with the clothes, working with colors and I did a good job. I knew when a certain scarf would be very fashionable and had to convince the company to buy a huge stock of this particular item.

The company had several showrooms in Europe and we had meetings together, too. My husband had a responsible job as well and travelled the world.

When my mother retired, she divorced my father. He made life very difficult for her to the point that they had to sell the house. We still worked together and she came to live with us for a year.

At the same time, our youngest son's teacher told us that he was acting different than the other children in class and we had to take him to a psychologist. From the time he could walk, he spent most of his time in the garden. He was not interested in TV or playing games, he loved being outside having a great time and he was very happy.

At school, he did not listen, even when the teachers told stories. Instead, he played with toys but did not speak. We thought he might be deaf and had his ears tested. His hearing was fine, so the specialist advised us to do some other tests. When we did, we were finally told he was autistic.

With my demanding job, my parents going through their ugly divorce, and my husband's travelling a lot, I fell apart. I was so tired, so stressed out. It was all too much.

One evening, I had to bring my oldest son to a karate lesson and we had to pass a hospital on the way. It was December, already dark, and it was raining. I did not see a woman crossing the street. She just came out of the hospital with her shoulder and arm in bandages and I almost hit her. Luckily, I missed her by a few inches. However, I was shocked and so was everybody else. I told my husband I could not live this hectic life any longer—things had to change. We agreed that I would give my resignation and my mother moved out to live in a condo above my brother's shop.

It was the beginning of a new millennium and a new path for me. The money monster showed up again, going from living on two incomes to one with the same bills every month.

Learning about autism and other labels, having a husband working hard to pay the bills, raising two boys and staying home, I had become what I was so frightened of—being dependent again and feeling guilty of not having an income of my own.

When our son was labelled autistic, we had to find another school and go where they advised so they could give him certain medications and treatments. Our son was not cooperative at all and I found it difficult to accept what the specialist told us. So we got more opinions and everyone told a different story. *Who was telling the truth?*

My mom saw me struggling and she took me to a lady who channeled Master Asaït. This was my first encounter with channeling and I did not know what to expect. I asked for a clear message in simple words about purpose and guidance and got a lot of information. The lady advised me that if I wanted to help my son, I should work on myself, and by doing so, I would help him. Sometimes, I listen to the tape of the session and am still amazed at how a simple message opens up a totally new world if you are open to change your point of view and explore what else is possible.

My mom also read an article in a magazine about the *Da Silva Alpha Training*. We took a workshop. I am very grateful she did this because it helped me a lot and still does.

Our brains function at different wave lengths, and when we are in the alpha wave state, just before we fall asleep or wake up, this is the wave which brings you in touch with the quantum field, the field of all possibilities and miracles.

I asked for help in paying the bills, for guidance with my children and things changed. Not always the way I expected it to be and we managed somehow. My son had to leave school and we got in touch with the Waldorf School (also known as the Rudolf Steiner School). Both our sons went to this new school and I also learned so many new things getting to know the teachings of Rudolf Steiner. These schools ask a lot of involvement from the parents, not like the traditional school, and you get to know the other children in the class and their parents.

Waldorf parents get tasks like cleaning the classrooms, helping with painting, and cleaning up the buildings of the school, preparing food and helping out with all kinds of events. These activities provide you a good bond with your children because you know their surroundings and you know what they are talking about.

Since my world was triggered so often with so many new thoughts and feelings, I learned new skills as well. I learned reflexology, being sensitive to the blocks and stuck energy in the body and the release when you can move them out.

In addition, I learned about Tachyon via the teachings and tools of Professor David Wagner, founder and CEO of Advanced Tachyon Technologies International (ATTI). He teaches you to live in verticality and be in the flow with the earth and the universe. This made a huge impact in my life and I am still using his products.

When the time came for my younger son to go to high school, we had a problem. He had developed well at the Waldorf School and was very visual and good with his hands. However, oral teachings and writing were difficult. So what to do next? Nobody could give us advice on any school. I've learned to be open with him. He has a will of his own and if I am open to that and follow what he is sending out, it will somehow unfold.

As it happened, I came into contact with a beautiful woman in Holland, a mystic who tapped into the Akashic Records to unfold the blueprint of the Age of Aquarius. She teaches about autism, dyslexia, and so many other "diseases" and "disabilities" and how these show up as we go from the Age of Pisces into the Age of Aquarius.

We learned so many new things about energy and light, including a meditation on how to protect our children on a daily basis. And a new school unfolded for my son. A Waldorf School in Antwerp was playing with the idea of opening a section for children like my son and so it happened. He went to Antwerp and he was one of 15 new pioneers in secondary school education.

You know, the money monster comes to visit at the darkest hour. When you know something needs to happen right now and you feel so alone, allow those feelings to be there, make your worst enemy your best friend, and do not doubt that help is always there. And if you are still afraid, keep asking for opportunities to show up, for more light and clearance to appear.

That same year, when my oldest son was 14, he had to do an assignment for school on the subject of metal. He had this vision that he wanted to forge a sword and save the world (like Aragon in *Lord of the Rings*). I asked for guidance and heard about a program on the radio where people can send in their wish and they would pick some of them. So I did and he got picked and was invited to the show and could tell his wish. One person answered and for several months, he could visit this person in his free time and learn how to forge his sword. What an amazing opportunity.

In March 2009, the money monster showed up big time. My husband lost his job and since this was the only source of income, what were we going to do? He had worked almost twenty years for this company; they let him go for no good reason and almost no severance pay.

My husband got so angry and frustrated and hired a lawyer to help him. Because he was so angry, he broke his ankle falling from a ladder while helping his sister and was not able to walk for three months. Our sons still went to school; we still had to pay our bills.

I already knew the story of Dr. Len and the *Ho'oponopono*. I found out that he was coming to Paris. So I went there as well. This beautiful, amazing teaching is not only about forgiving yourself, but by forgiving yourself, you clean the land you live on, the house you live in, the furniture you sit on, the neighborhood you live in and everyone involved. You are born being a miracle and you have the right to live your amazing life here on earth and so it was created.

Through eons of time there has been so much struggle and despair but our planet has this amazing ability to heal if we ask her and give her the permission to do so. If we could all be Jesus and put our hand on someone or something and all "disease" and "stuck energies" could be transformed and transmuted to its original state of the divine blueprint.

The prayers of the *Ho'oponopono* helped a lot. My husband received his severance pay and my mother, who had struggled for years with the paperwork of her pension, found someone who fixed it all and she received her pension. My husband applied for a job in France—not easy being over fifty—and got the job.

We lived in Belgium, and now were being asked to move to France, which made our sons unhappy. I learned about the tools of

Access Consciousness, the Clearing Statement and the Bars. This is to ask questions and clear all the energies and emotions that come up when asking the questions.

Moving from one country to another takes a lot of work: new laws, insurance, healthcare, housing, taxes, banks, language, culture and food. We had several vacations in France and even though both countries are in the European Union, they are very different.

I remember once participating in a sweat lodge and a ceremony by Native Americans. On the day it happened, I got my period and was invited to have a meditation outside in nature and connect with the moon. In the Native Americans' way of life, when a woman has her period, she is in direct contact with her spirits and has a very strong energy that can disturb other ceremonies. That is why they have to stay outside the village. Not because a woman having her period is a bad thing, but because it helps her grow stronger and become more aware of herself and able to help the medicine man healing others.

So I followed their instructions and got this clear vision how important it is to have a solid foundation—man, woman and child. How important it is to feel safe and to be nurtured and vulnerable.

So finally my husband and I moved to France. He has his job and I have to create a whole new journey. I attended the "Embody Your Higher Self" retreat with Rikka Zimmerman in Hawaii and went swimming with the dolphins. I received an invitation from Anne Deidre with a discount on a reading as a birthday gift. I did not know her, but my intuition told me to go for it—Anne showed me a way of getting "out there." And so this is part of my next step and sharing my story.

Writing this story and going through all these hidden emotions and feelings, I always asked for more guidance and input about my father's motivation in writing the letter I shared with you at the beginning of this chapter. Suddenly, it all became so clear. He observed me doing my best to live in gratitude and seeing the best in people on a daily basis. My father saw in me what I see in others—the greatness to be able to touch people's hearts and inviting me to tap into that greatness and not in fear, what I chose when I was 22 years old.

Receiving this insight opened up so big and released a lot of fear and choosing a small life.

Thank you for taking the time to read my story.

May your life be blessed with your own love, your own support, and your own connection to your Higher Self.

Becky Henderson, M. Ed.

Becky Henderson M. Ed. is a mother, a Transformational Author, Entrepreneur, and a Master Teacher. She has joined forces with Happy Publishing and is one of the authors in the book, 365 *Days of Inspirational Animal Messages.* Her forthcoming book is titled *My Art of Resiliency*, where she describes more in detail her prison experience.

Becky is a certified Angel Card Reader, a certified Law of Attraction Basic Practitioner, a Level 1 Hand Analyst Trained in Fingerprint Identification, and has a certificate of completion of twenty-hour of hypnosis training with emphasis on self-hypnosis, age regression and past life regression. In addition, she is a certified Reiki 1 and 2 practitioner.

Becky works with clients with a mastery of modalities that serves her clients understanding of their spiritual purpose and mission on earth. With divine and angelic guidance, her clients are empowered to connect with deeper aspects of themselves and helps them move forward with power and purpose. Becky offers Angel Readings and coaching programs and as a past life regression mentor, she will assist you in understanding where you have been so that you can move forward more powerfully into the future and live the life of your dreams.

Contact Information:
Website: www.beckyhendersonauthor.com
Email: hendersonbecky1@gmail.com

Amazing Grace

By Becky Henderson, M.Ed.

*I*t was March 12, 1998 when my phone rang in my motel room in San Diego, California. I answered the phone and it was my friend calling from Wyoming. He told me that my funeral had just taken place. He described it more like an event than a funeral. He described which family members were there, who stood out as a friend possibly, and most importantly, all of the Department of Criminal Investigators and Federal Agents who were scattered among the place.

My oldest brother was heard saying, "This funeral is a joke." It was so surreal as I sat on my motel room bed facing the air conditioner thinking, "This is really happening. I can never go back . . . I am officially dead."

Well, I did end up going back, just not to my luxurious life. Quite the opposite—a gang of jail cells and home became my Maximum Security Federal Prison cell.

Rewind a few years earlier when I was being trailed by the government because I was associating with a drug dealer. I was living the dream, a paid-off business that was thriving, a new custom-built home in the mountains, and I ask myself, "Why? Why would I risk everything just to babysit for a drug dealer?"

It is definitely not who I am today. It sounds crazy now, so much has changed, especially me.

Three months after my funeral, the Feds did end up catching up with me after I had faked my own death. My initial charge was a conspiracy drug charge. In other words, I was charged for a crime that the drug dealer committed, even though I was nowhere near him when someone wore a wire on him while he was selling drugs. The collapse of his operation took me and four others down with him.

Conspiracy is not hard to prove. All it takes is two or more people saying something illegal took place, or two or more people in the same room when something illegal is taking place, and somebody in that room tells the authorities. The drug dealer said he weighed out his drugs at my house while dropping off the children one day. That earned him many years off of his sentence, while putting years on mine.

My high-dollar lawyer told me that if I fought against the United States of America, I would surely lose and then my sentence would even be longer. She explained to me that around 90 percent of criminal defendants end up pleading guilty. In most cases, defendants who do take their cases all the way to court and end up losing at a Federal trial are punished severely by the judge. The defendant ends up with the maximum sentence, not the minimum.

Not having any priors and a history of being a productive, law-abiding citizen did not make any difference at all—Federal mandatory minimum guidelines are what dictate your sentence. Your prosecutor determines your sentence by looking at a chart. Welcome to the "war on drugs," where even law-abiding citizens go down at the drop of a hat.

I was already facing ten years to life . . . no wonder I chose to run. I did have the option of committing suicide; I had the perfect gun for it. Thank God the person who helped me fake my death talked me out of that idea. It was either death or prison in my eyes—running would at least give me a few more days, months, or maybe even years of freedom. I guess you could say that I was extremely scared. I had never been in trouble before and now was in a panicked state of mind.

By the time the Federal Marshalls found me, I was just a walking shell. I was a negative numbed-out corpse, still walking around. It was almost a relief when they asked me to give them my name and social security number, I couldn't get it out any sooner. At the same time, I could feel my legs getting really warm and wet. My plan of forcing them to shoot me by pretending to point a gun at them or running away failed. Instead, my resistance turned into such a broken state that I relieved myself by urinating on myself.

This would set the scene for the next five days while in a small cell with ten or more other people. We shared a cement floor with no pillow, no blanket. We shared a water fountain, or should I say we swapped spit, as you had to suck the water out of the hole to get any water out of it. My shorts were wet, I was cold, I was broken. I had hit the bottom of the septic tank; I was now a full-fledged prisoner.

I thought about asking for a phone call to my mother, but I knew that she was at peace, knowing that I had run and was living a life without prison walls. As for my siblings—heck, they helped get the grand jury to put out the warrant, so why would they care if I was really alive? They had buried me a long time ago. So, I did nothing.

Finally, on about the fourth day in a Las Vegas jail, I was handed a pencil, three pieces of paper, and a stamped envelope. Something told me to write my mother and tell her that I had been arrested. The moment I started writing "*Dear Mom . . .*", another inmate felt the need to make fun of me because I was writing to my "mommy." Who else was I going to write to? I had no one and no one cared whether I was alive or dead.

I did not know it at the time but the news had already hit my hometown the day I had been arrested. I was on the news, on the front page of the local paper, and was told later that I was even on *America's Most Wanted* and *Unsolved Mysteries*! My mother had already started the process of getting my truck and camper out of repo and returning what was left of my life back to her house. I felt the Universe pulling me out of the ocean that I was drowning in.

Eventually, I was moved to a Federal facility where I could receive items for hygiene such as a Q-tip. While going to sleep at night, I found myself thanking God for my bed, my pillow, the roof over my head, and the food in my stomach. Grace started coming into my life slowly. I used that grace to get me through the next year.

I was moved to Seattle, Washington, then to Oklahoma City, Oklahoma . . . all on Conair where no one cares if your seat belt is on. Only the marshals get to wear seatbelts, while we prisoners were handcuffed and trying to eat bologna sandwiches out of brown paper bags. I would gaze out the window and hope for a sign of winter . . . snow perhaps. The Feds never tell the prisoners where they are going. If they did, the chances of prisoners trying to escape increases. Every time there was a plane change, men with guns surrounded the planes just in case a prisoner ran.

Finally, the day came and the plane landed in Wyoming. I was told that it was Wyoming, but where was the snow? I was told that it was now summer, the snow was gone. Who would know? We were not told anything while being expedited to our original state of arrest. On my way through booking, one deputy told me that I would get an automatic five years for just "escaping." I watched that little spirit I had built up just fly out of my body and sweep away. I knew that I was doomed.

When I was moved to a cell, I could not believe how small everything was. Only four cells, two tables to eat on, and no place to exercise. I had found hell and did not even have to die. Just when I thought things were getting better, things got worse.

I spent most of my time in my cell crying while MTV was blaring on the television all managed by the pod bully. No one got a say in what was watched on television unless you wanted to fight the pod bully. It was not that important to me, I just wanted to die . . . again.

I sat in that jail cell for ten months. Thank God for food—otherwise my broken spirit would have had nothing to live for. By the time my sentencing came, my body had become a 180 lb. spiritless blob. My mom hardly recognized me at my first day of trial.

The trial turned into a very short session. A few disgruntled employees I had fired for embezzlement appeared eager and ready to say anything the government wanted them to say. I had a new lawyer, as I could not afford the high-dollar one I had before I ran. She fought so hard for me, but we were not getting anywhere, so I finally gave in and pled guilty. I received a 57-month sentence in a Federal prison. The last man standing was furious with me. As the dominoes go down, they go down, and so did he.

Off to prison I went.

I had been living with the same three girls, minus the Shepherd case, in which two girls were arrested for murder after the fact. That was when Wyoming got its first "Hate Crime Law." Those same three girls were wearing on my last nerve.

When I heard someone say, "Henderson, pack up," I knew I was on to a better place. I got loaded into that small plane that was taking me "somewhere," and right next to me was one of my three cellies.

I looked at her and said, "I am so tired of living with you, why are you still here?" She didn't know any better than I where we were going. Finally, the security said, "You Dublin."

I heard one of the guys say, "Hey, that is where Heidi Fleiss is! You are so lucky you will be seeing a star!" Heidi was the "Hollywood Madame" who became a TV and radio celebrity.

I had no idea who she was but was grateful when they said that my cellie would be going to a "camp" where the so-called non-violent inmates went. In reality, she was the only one who was violent, head-butting others on a regular basis in our last facility.

When I was processed through booking, I got to do a new head shot, formerly known as a mug shot. There I was, 192 lbs., almost twice the person I used to be. Only no person existed in me; I was only a shell.

The first night I had the bottom bunk and had to listen to the girls on the top bunk doing things that were forbidden in a prison facility. The next day, I scrubbed showers and was told by the "lifers" that my work was not good enough and so I had to do it again. I guess you could say I had definitely hit the bottom of the septic tank.

I was put into a cell with two others and settled in a few weeks after R & R (receiving and releasing). I was forced to get a job at 12 cents an hour. I chose to teach GED and work in the library. By grace, the Bureau of Prisons (B.O.P.) accepted me into that department. I was able to run on the track when I wasn't working.

Slowly, I started to feel like who I was again. Grace was coming everywhere I would seek. With letters coming from home and friends, phone calls, money in my commissary, and the best part was the books that were sent to me from my mother, I knew that I could survive by being thankful for these things, and I was.

The holidays, birthdays, and work days all went by. They were all "another" day. My cellie would tell me that she had "eight" Christmases to go, and I felt so grateful that I didn't get a 20-year sentence like she did. She was a drug dealer's girlfriend who had gone down for him . . . seemed it was going around, only I wasn't the girlfriend.

My 57-month sentence was nothing compared to these girls; some of them were in there for killing their own children. It was a maximum security prison. I was not surprised when I came across women who killed.

It was ironic when I was approached by another inmate asking me if I wanted to take the empty bed in their room. It just happened to be Heidi Fleiss's bed, who I never was introduced to. It felt so good to be wanted by someone, I said yes right away.

My new cellies introduced me into a whole new "club fed" world, a world full of massages, pedicures, manicures, and your laundry done once a week. As long as you had the money, you could get these services, everybody had a hustle. My favorite one was the cheesecake. Another inmate made the best cheesecake I had ever tasted, all supplied by the kitchen via stolen food.

The more I was grateful for, the more the Universe brought to me. Pretty soon, I had a job in the recreation center, where I mopped floors and lifted weights. I could walk/run the yard while I was working . . . my outer shell started disappearing before my eyes. Slowly but surely, I was turning back into Becky.

My release day came and I was transferred to a half-way house in Wyoming. I didn't care that it was just a different form of an institution, as long as I was closer to my home, which was about six hours away. I got a job immediately at the local mall as a security officer. I couldn't believe that I was in charge of a huge mall's security while living in a half-way house.

The Universe was giving me more and more; this gift was the gift of being "trustworthy again". And the gifts just kept on coming. Next, I was able to have a friend transport my truck to me. Wow! I was able to have my own vehicle, the vehicle I was arrested in twice. Goes to show you that everything that rings true is not exactly true. You see, when you are dealing drugs or have drugs on you, your vehicle is the first thing that they take. In my circumstance, I always owned my truck; in fact, I still have it today.

Back Home Where I Belong

The day came when I was released to go home. Where was home? I had already sold my house and property, so home would have to be at my mother's house. It was a long drive home, but as soon as I saw the property, I knew I was safe. I was almost expecting a banner that read "WELCOME HOME, BECKY HENDERSON! YOU ARE WELCOME HERE!"

But no, I heard someone in the distance saying, "Shut the gate." It was my step-father who hated me, resented me, was jealous of me, and had told the Federal agents lies to get me put away in jail. Oh well, at least I was home. I just needed to find a way to stay safe.

I knew that life on the outside would be full of surprises, but several things really stood out. Things that I noticed the most were that everyone had a cell phone pasted to their faces, and most were carrying a laptop computer. Money looked like Monopoly play money to me for some reason. I also had a real hard time shopping for items at the stores. There were so many items to choose from. I was not used to making my own choices, and forgot how for a while.

It felt good to be free but living in one of my mother's rooms made me feel like a loser. To help me feel more grateful for how far I had gone, I pulled my journal out from my days in prison. What caught my eye was the page of collected works of the things that I missed. This is what I had written:

- I miss feeling sheets against me as I sleep.

- I miss being able to go to the bathroom when I need to, and without an audience.

- I miss taking a shower without my shoes on.

- I miss taking a bath.

- I miss knowing what size clothes I wear.

- I miss seeing myself in a mirror.

- I miss feeling carpet on my bare feet.

- I miss petting a dog.

- I miss hearing the river roar.

- I miss seeing the creeks flow.

- I miss my old body.

- I miss hearing silence.

- I miss hearing children laugh.

- I miss hearing a phone ring.

- I miss hearing the snow crunch underneath my feet.

And then I went on to say that I enjoy warmth because I have been cold; I appreciate the light because I have been in darkness; I experience joy because I have known sorrow; I want to love because I have lived through so much hate.

Now I had all of those things and was I forever grateful for them. I was on supervised release, which meant that I had a probation officer and was drug tested quite often. This would go on for the next five years. I have to admit that I hid out for a very long time. It was very shameful to move back to the county in which I had been under surveillance and arrested. I felt like scum . . . again. It was hard to hold my head up tall and just carry on, but I managed to do it.

It helped that I started taking classes at the local college. Eventually, I earned an associate's degree in business management. I met someone special and we had a baby. I felt real authentic happiness that came from the inside—not some superficial happiness that depended on how much "stuff" I owned. I learned the hard way that "stuff" can be taken away from anybody at any time. Education and authenticity cannot be taken away from anyone.

I now live in the moment. In the past, I was so busy running my business, building my house, paying off my land and business, and planning my retirement that I forgot to live.

I have learned to live in the moment, mostly from my daughter. I savored every moment with her and still do. While raising my daughter, I eventually earned my bachelor's degree in social science and then went on to receiving my master's degree in education.

I spend a lot of time trying to heal from the past by watching many teleseminars on the computer that are spiritually uplifting. At first, I studied the Universal Laws and started living by them. This led to all kinds of different venues where I could better myself with the hopes of helping others. The best thing about all of this spiritual knowledge coming my way was it was all for free!

This path also led me to Anne, the lady who gave me this opportunity to get my story out to help others in some way. Some of the people in the transformational field I idolized started becoming my friends and colleagues. The more I surrounded myself with people who were like-minded and people I could learn from, the more opportunities came to me in order to live my passion. Eventually I earned a Law of Attraction Practitioner Certificate, Angel Card Reader Certificate, and completed a Level 1 Hand Analysts training in fingerprint identification. All of these tools were not only to help myself find my passion, but to help others as well.

My awakening to grace was just a matter of allowing a new world of motivations to work within me. I could not *think* my way into a new way of living; I had to *live* my way into a new way of thinking. I became someone who made choices with a conscious mind.

Looking back at everything I went through, I can still see grace. I met many interesting people in the prison system, some guilty and some not so guilty, but all interesting. I learned about the justice system inside and out, which gave me more compassion for what others have to go through when they are accused of a crime. If I had not been forced to sell my business and my house, I most likely would never have gone back to school and get a great education. So, if anything, I am grateful for the person I have become today due to all of these life experiences.

I share with you my story to show you that no matter where you come from—wealth, poverty, or even prison—you can transform your life for the better. So, if you find yourself making an unconscious choice or choosing a behavior that leads to consequences, know that every day is a new day with new choices.

This chapter is just a preview of what is to come in my next book. In my forthcoming book, *My Art of Resiliency*, you can read in more detail about what led me to become a fugitive, how I planned my fake suicide, and my experiences in the justice system. There is much more to tell that I could have never fit in one chapter.

With that being said, if you need a little Angel Therapy/ Healing, I am here to help you. Until then, love yourself unconditionally, believe in your dreams and know that you are a magnet to Divine abundance and guidance each and every day.

Becky Henderson was presented the Editor's Choice Award by The International Library of Poetry for two years in a row in 1998 and 1999. She has had several poems published, but the following one describes best her perseverance and spiritual awakening.

Blessings in Disguise

This is the story about blessings in disguise:
They come in different ways, making them hard to recognize.
You will find them quite surprising and a little odd,
But later on you will see it is an amazing act of God.

My arrest seemed like a tragedy after I had run;
Instead, God was just closing a door, but He opened another one.
I thought I was through living, after I accomplished all my dreams;
Another life was waiting for me, though it seems.

My material wealth vanished right before my eyes,
While I sat in jail fighting all of the lies.
Before I knew it, God was my best friend;
Spirituality and faith is what he would recommend.

The winds of life blew new air and took away the hurt;
In time, prayer became a source of strength and comfort.
This miraculous turnabout is evidence of a spiritual awakening;
My blessing was the gift of faith, no matter what the future might bring.

This is another one of Becky's published poems:

The Family That Prays Together, Stays Together

Would it be asking too much to have a real family?
Not just in my dreams, but a family I could see.
One that stays together, through thick and through thin,
Knowing that anything else would be the same as a sin.
A brother that would protect me and show me the way;
He would be so proud of me, he could never betray.
A sister I could call, when I needed a friend;
Her advice she would give, her clothes she would lend.
Our father would take us to church every Sunday,
Smiling and holding my hand all the way.
Mom would be so happy, surrounded by all this loyalty.
A family that prayed together, that's what we would be!

When I get to Heaven, I want to be able to say to God,
"I gave all of the gifts You gave to me to others."

Catherine M. Laub

Catherine M. Laub is an Author, Speaker, Professional Psychic Medium, and a Spiritual Guide & Consultant. She is highly gifted in psychically delivering information to people from the spiritual realm and their guides and angels that benefits them greatly with their lives.

Catherine is a spiritual and inspirational workshop facilitator and does readings at local events, as well as performing sessions with clients worldwide, via phone and Skype, email and in person. She is a Priestess with Goddess energy and studied the natural rhythms of Earth, Water, Air, Fire and Spirit and adds these rhythms to her readings.

Catherine is a 5-time bestselling author and continues her writing in upcoming anthologies. These stories are about her healing and spiritual journeys. Catherine speaks about mental illness in her campaign "Brighten Your Day with Turquoise", where she shares her own journey with mental illness and a suicide attempt. Here she guides others to feel invigorated and empowered to go forward in their own struggles. She believes you can do anything if you put your mind to it. Catherine's message is that you are not alone and there is a support system waiting for you.

Catherine loves to do jigsaw puzzles and play bingo with her mother at local bingo halls. Whenever she gets the chance she travels for vacation and business. The rest of her time is spent with her husband Tony, 7 children and 14 grandchildren. Joshua is her closest because he loves to visit and play with Gama.

Contact Information:

Website: www.catherinemlaub.com
Email: catherinemlaub@gmail.com
www.facebook.com/catherine.laub.54
https://www.linkedin.com/in/catherinemlaub

It's All In The Journey

By Catherine M. Laub

*I*t's not just about the destination. It is about the journey! As written on a birthday card from my mother.

I help people gain the knowledge they are seeking to begin or continue on their spiritual journey and am supportive of those who are suffering with a mental illness.

My journey has been challenging at times and now it is all good thanks to the guidance of my angels. I am an empath, meaning I'm a sensitive person and everything affects me, both physically and psychologically. Because of this, I had to make some choices that some people may think to be extreme.

I was in really bad shape with my physical and mental health August, 2014 and attempted suicide. I felt like there was a wall up and it wasn't me going through the actions. While in the hospital, I was interviewed by a psychiatric staff with 20 students in attendance because of the complex nature of my health symptoms. They realized I was a package deal, not only the mental, because it and the physical work off each other.

I am still being seen by psychiatric professionals and will possibly be necessary most of my life. I learned too many times that even with the help of the doctors, it was difficult to stop taking my antidepressants. I will proceed with caution when I am ready to be weaned off my medications. I am leaving it up to God and my angels to guide me with this. It is a personal journey for each of us and requires our own professional team.

At that time, my angel community did a Tarot card reading for me and when I heard it, I realized that I was lonely. Tony and I lived together but didn't spend time with one another. He was working full-time from our house as a salesman and I was spending time with my lessons and mostly watching TV.

I believe the only way to lead my life is through authenticity. Sometimes my authenticity is too much because I tell it like it is. That sometimes causes turmoil with others.

My therapist, Patricia Firestone in Holbrook, New York, has tried for many years to help me realize that some of my health issues were due to my sensitivity and I absorbed other people's negativity and energy. How I absorbed these issues was both mental and physical. The physical was with what I call my "disposal system," for I had suffered with bladder issues since early child-hood and from colitis and IBS since I began fifth grade.

I was told to squash my talk and it wreaked havoc on my health. The thyroid is in the throat chakra and is related to our speech and communication. My sister lectured me, "Nobody wants to hear you are sick. Stop telling people that." That's when I started having severe thyroid problems. It took years to get my thyroid to a fairly healthy point, and now that I am not connected with my siblings and live my life authentically, I am better. My siblings ganged up against me twice and made me feel both unloved and attacked. The same sister told me I had to apologize because I was the one who was wrong.

I always felt different than my siblings and not loved as much as them. They treated me differently all my life and always seemed to team up against me. Because of this, I learned it is better to end my relationships with all of them. This revelation was in December 2011. Along with the five of them, I also stopped talking with my parents. This was the hardest because I was always close to my mother and I loved listening to my father's war stories.

I remember the last time I visited with my father while he was still healthy. He showed me all his army medals and ribbons and how he displayed them in a framed glass case. He also had a photo album that none of us ever saw, not even my mother; and they had been married over 50 years by then. It was photos of him and his army buddies, including General Dwight D. Eisenhower; my father was his driver during the war. I was honored because he chose me to share it with. He asked me to be sure when he died to display these items in the funeral home for all to see. We followed his wishes and it was a wonderful tribute to him.

My struggles with my siblings always made me feel like the "black sheep" of the family. In talking with my therapist, I learned that most empathic and sensitive people feel the same way. It is because we are different so we get treated differently.

In May 2014, I read an advice column by Elise Solé that essentially told the writer that she was a horrible person because of the things she wrote. This is a summary: she excluded her sister from family functions and said "Her life is quite different from ours. We're not interested in what she has to talk about. She complains too much about her aches and pains, and claims to have some kind of neurological disease that some of us feel is more psychosomatic than real."

My being the "uninvited sister" started way back in 1992 when my husband left me and my 3 small children. Nine months later, one of my sisters lost her husband at age 33. So even though I was in a state of shock and depressed, my family said I have nothing to complain about, that a death is worse than anything and she is all alone. My parents stayed at her house for months helping her out.

Tony, my husband now, actually had to tell my mother many years ago that a divorce is similar to a death because you are still left alone and especially having three kids to care for and being on welfare. So my sister was catered to while I was left hanging. She is the same one who talked badly about me to my kids and thought she was superior to me even though she is two years younger.

I have co-authored five books talking about my illnesses and spirituality. I will continue doing so to share with others that as much as we go through in our lives we can overcome anything we put our minds to.

My psychic-medium skills have advanced far beyond anything I could imagine. When I started doing psychic fairs, I was afraid to call myself a psychic. I learned quickly that what I was doing was considered more than just intuition, as I was calling it. I have always been spiritual and searching for my niche. I grew into my spirituality.

While my three children were growing up, I attended mass often with them. When my ex-husband left us and I was left to care for all three alone, it was a little harder for a while. I worked full time and was solely responsible to get them to dance and their sports events. We moved in with Tony in 1993, but I felt like it was up to me to raise my own kids. He had already raised his own daughter and three step-daughters. It became harder to attend mass, but eventually I joined a prayer group. I also became a religious education teacher for Vanessa's class. (Vanessa is my youngest daughter.) I did that for two years until I fell apart mentally over a personal problem.

I signed up for many different classes in a variety of fields. Among them were spiritual-based and self-help-related classes. I have been working with Anne Deidre for over a year and she has helped me realize a lot of my skills. In February 2015, Anne prompted me to do a medium reading for her. I had never done that and was surprised at the visions I had and the messages I was able to give to Anne. Since then, my gift has expanded and while doing readings, I get many messages from beyond. I get goosebumps as confirmation that I am being accurate during my readings

I love everything spiritual. When I'm able to give a message, I am thrilled as I'm helping someone. It all amazes me. My readings are always accurate and I'm thanked for the insights I give.

As a child and growing up, I could see spirits and only recently learned they were angels and possibly relatives who had passed and are with me on my journey. I visited my grandparents every summer with my family and saw many spirits at their home throughout my life.

In 1985, when Hurricane Gloria hit Long Island, NY, I lived in my in-laws' basement. We lost power for several days and didn't have windows to let any light in. For two nights, when I lay down to sleep, a wall of light from floor to ceiling appeared at the foot of my bed. I couldn't see through this light. I took it to be a message from someone that my father's upcoming open heart surgery was going to be a success. This is just something I sensed at the time. But as time went on, I realized I had been receiving messages all along.

I receive many signs from the spirit world. Feathers appear in the most unusual places and while working with Anne Deidre, I asked her "what's with all the feathers?" She proceeded to explain they were from her mother. In response, Anne was amazed because she remembered seeing many feathers in her yard that day.

While on the phone, she gathered them, then put them in a bowl and sent me a picture. More recently, she described finding a white ball of feathers in her mother's house. It wasn't anything she saw before and now knew it was confirmation her mother is guiding her.

Two incidences took place in my home with my father-in-law. While talking to a friend about him, a hanging stemmed glass flew off my wall unit and burst into pieces. He confirmed his presence. This was Tony's father and he didn't believe me because at that time he was a non-believer. About a year later, Tony and I were discussing his father and the same thing happened. This time he believed my connections to the spirit world.

For many years, I saw a beautiful woman just hanging out in the top corner of my bedroom as I went to sleep. After learning more about angels, I finally realized she was one of my angel guides. There have been many of these spirits in my home and it was always a source of fright. Today, I welcome and acknowledge them.

Spirits are always speaking through signs. You can learn more in my free report, 7 *WAYS TO KNOW YOUR ANGELS AND LOVED ONES IN SPIRIT ARE WITH YOU* on my website.

In 2011, I was taking in-person spiritual lessons in a small group with a local reverend, Pat. At one of these circles, I had my first spirit visitation during a meditation that totally scared me. Five spirits visited me. I started to cry and at first fought it. Finally, I burst into tears. I asked what messages they had but I was scared.

After the meditation, I blurted out that I saw all of these people. My teacher said, "That's great! What a breakthrough." I explained what I saw and how the tears overpowered me. They were all smiling widely before saying anything then they clarified it was my first spirit connection and it was a great one. I described bouncing around from our place to upstate then to the living room. I felt flushed from head to toe, plus my legs and body were shaking.

Pat told me not to be scared and the crying was just my soul being excited. This played a very important part in my spirituality.

That same night, I saw a quick vision of a tree that brought me to "my tree," which I saw in my first meditation years ago. It represents the Tree of Life. I then saw myself leaning on it and sliding down and connecting with the ground. I saw the big field around me. One woman believed I was grounding myself. We then worked with "seeing" each other's messages.

When I worked with a man, Pete, I heard a small dog behind me outside and I brought his energy across for healing to Pete. Afterwards, I asked if anyone else heard and only he did. He joked how it was yelping. I didn't see anything with the other woman but I saw something with Pat, the teacher. I realized when I got home that there was a connection for me. I saw a railroad tunnel that was dark and got brighter toward the end. I realized at home that Popop, my grandfather, worked on the railroad. I believe he was there waiting to help the others come through for me.

When I was leaving, Pat told me she was happy for me and it was a great first time. I said, "Now I have to try harder and concentrate on everyone else." She said no, just go with it and let it happen.

I couldn't sleep every night after then. I was now open and it allowed spirits to visit me. I woke up and saw them lining up from the opposite corner of the room. It was like in the movie *Ghost*, where the psychic saw people coming through the walls demanding to be heard. They wanted my help but I was too tired to help at that time. I learned how to turn off my abilities so I could sleep. I did this and for a couple years, I turned off most of my abilities. My gifts are finally getting stronger every day.

Jump to the year 2012. My father continued to have heart problems and a couple more heart attacks. In January 2012, in a dream, he told me he wouldn't live past the end of the year. We had a few setbacks with him throughout the year. Then the first week of December, he came to me in another dream. He looked into my eyes and said, "Please just let me die."

When he ended up in the emergency room with pneumonia a few days later, I had to see him immediately. My husband and I both kissed him goodbye knowing it might be the last time we would see him. He was getting better and two days later, he was having a great visit with a friend. Right after that, he had a massive heart attack and was dead for 20 minutes. After he was revived, he was in a coma and never came out of it. My mother and entire family made the decision to let him go four days later. There were 23 of us with him.

My father appeared to me a few days after that, standing at the foot of my bed, just smiling at me. After that, he visited me nightly. I never saw him in full body again, but his energy field was so strong that I knew he was sitting in the chair watching over me. He now comes to me very often in my dreams and through messages from other intuitives. I even "saw" him walking on the sidewalks of New York in August of 2014. He tilted his head to me as if to say, "Yes, I am Daddy." His message is how proud he is of me and he is continuing to guide me through my journey to help others.

I studied Angel Communication through Angels Teach University, where I received two certifications. Reverend Elvia and her teachers and students are all great people. They are always there for me if I need someone to talk to. I was introduced to the Angels Teach circle through a life coach.

While visiting my brother-in-law before my first Hay House event and after reviewing the schedule of speakers, he stated that he had a friend who does spiritual work. I contacted her. She guided me toward moving forward from my negative position. She talked me through the negativity and drew an Angel card to do a short reading. Then she walked me through a meditation. It was great. When I learned how simple it was to take lessons from Angels Teach, I signed up immediately. Donna Cantone is one of the people who is always there for me.

I have a campaign to bring support to those with mental illness, "Brighten Your Day with Turquoise." My angels gave me this mission and said to use turquoise because it is the color for healing and has a calming effect. Please visit my website for more information about the color turquoise.

I am gathering resources to share with anyone who wishes to obtain help and guidance in their journey. Eventually I will open a store/retreat where I will sell spiritual, self-help and inspirational items. I will have a living room setting for people to come relax when having a stressful day. There will be a jigsaw puzzle set up welcoming anyone to work on. Next to that an area for creation journaling and vision board making. I will have handouts covering various areas of mental illness and self-help that will guide people to feeling better. Soothing music will be playing and books will be there to be read while sitting. Workshops will be held in various capacities.

I realize the road is rocky but it has to be to gain experience. My goal is to help people gain the knowledge they are seeking to begin or continue on their spiritual and healing journey. Additionally to help them achieve their potential without all the obstacles that get in the way. I have many health challenges and am guiding others with similar ones. Since I have already gone through enough of them I know what to watch out for. My message for everyone is have faith and know you can always pull through anything!!!

I am ... I can ... I do ...

Melissa Le Blanc

Melissa LeBlanc built her company up from ground zero to 6 figures in just over a year. Melissa is the Thriving Mama Business Mentor for busy moms. She loves to inspire and help other moms to make it to six figures from the comfort of their homes by focusing on time management, success strategy, and breaking through blocks and limited beliefs keeping them from their highest money success. As a mother of 5 littles, entrepreneur, mentor, and wife, Melissa understands how to help moms break through the struggle of life/ work balance and create thriving success in life and business that supports their biggest role as a mom. As the go-to expert in her field, Melissa's mission is helping moms everywhere liberate their family & business life so they can truly be living a life they love and leaving a legacy of success!

She is also the CEO and Founder of Healing for Wholeness, Mamas Making Money and the Co-Founder of The Prosperity Approach, as well as a Certified Simply Healed Energy Practitioner, and Global Summit Host. She loves to spend quality time with her family laughing, camping, playing games, going on adventures and making a difference.

Please visit www.melissaleblanc.com and receive a FREE GIFT: The Busy Mom's Productivity Toolkit- Hit your goals in half the time; the ultimate resource to take back your time so you can take back your life.

Contact Information:

Website: www.melissaleblanc.com
Email: support@melissaleblanc.com

Holding Self Back Because of Limitation, Fear, and People-Pleasing

By Melissa LeBlanc

I've always had it in me. You might even know what I'm talking about. That voice. The pull. The call. That whisper in the silence that says there is greatness in me, in you, that we are made for more.

According to my mom, I was an eager child, ready to jump at every opportunity, including birth. I was so anxious to get here that my mother was wheeled into the delivery room within minutes of arriving at the hospital. I arrived earlier than my due date and was delivered by two nurses before the doctor could even get there. Apparently, I was ready and anxious for whatever this life had to offer.

On my first birthday, my mom felt there was something "off" with me despite my happy, bubbly nature. The doctors ran some tests and discovered there was, in fact, a problem. It all came crashing down and suddenly made sense.

There was a reason I was tilting my head and running into walls. I was legally blind. Not only that, but I had a number of diagnoses that went along with the blindness: albinism, nystagmus, strabismus, and astigmatism. All pretty much revealing that my life would not be normal.

Questions of "How did this happen? Was there a cause?" flooded my mother's thoughts. The doctors confirmed that a rare combination of genes from my mom and dad contributed to this specific genetic disorder.

Then, my brother was born one year later. They discovered the same thing with him, except his was worse. I remember going to pick him up from The School of the Blind when I was six years old. They were always doing fun activities, inviting him to special events, and giving him special gadgets and tools to see better. Because he was worse than I, he received a lot of special treatment—including free stuff and attention. He even got a new computer from my aunts and uncles when we were in elementary school.

I always wondered why I wasn't special enough. Why I didn't get the same kind of attention and treatment? Maybe I wasn't good enough or bad enough, however you look at it. What was all the fuss about anyway? I played it off as if none of it mattered. I stayed silent. I pretended it was all good. After all, I could pull off looking fairly normal. That is, except in the summer time when I had to go outside in long-sleeved shirts, with a hat, sunglasses and lathered up in sunscreen). If I didn't keep up that geeked up "dress code," I would get sunburnt and blistered. I passed out easily if I wasn't hydrated or was in the sun too long, and that would follow with a major migraine for hours afterwards.

Nonetheless, I did NOT want be one of those kids who got laughed at and gawked at because she was different. I did everything I could to appear normal. I felt I was doing a good job most of the time until annoying people would come up to my mom and say something like "what cute little 'towheads.'" Oh, please. I never got it until I learned what that meant. Hehe.

Anyhow, my brother eventually left the School for The Blind and went back to normal public school like me. Things were different for him there. He got teased and made fun of. He also had strabismus like me, but his was more obvious. I was able to get surgery for mine because mine was a different type. My eyes turned outward, his turned inward. Yes, he was a true cross-eyed.

It broke my heart to see people being so insensitive when they would cross their eyes and make faces and call out his name. One day I had enough. I ran toward this particular bully named Tyler. I rammed my head into his gut and then flipped him over my shoulder into the ditch. The name-calling and making fun of stopped for a bit. I felt like a hero.

Even though I was always protecting my brother and being his advocate, most peers and adults didn't know I struggled with some of the same issues. I had feelings of shame and embarrassment and the yearning to actually be normal like everybody else. Sitting in the front of the classroom got old. When I sat at the back of the class, I couldn't see anything on the chalkboard and would have to listen very intently to learn.

I did my best to hide my afflictions. That's why I would sit in the back of the classroom and refused to wear glasses. People treated me differently otherwise, as if I was diseased or something. If any of my friends found out, all of a sudden they would talk more softly, asking if this or that was okay to do. Ugh. So I didn't let this "limitation" stop me. I had confidence, courage and somehow had an incredible belief in myself to do things just like everyone else.

Then I got older.

I loved to run, I was good at it, too. In junior high, I decided to try out for track. I knew I'd make the team because I was the fastest girl in my entire class. In fact, the coach was begging me to try out so I could be on the relay team. He called me his "little runner girl." I was so proud of that and he was proud of me.

That all shattered the day he laid into me when I had to quit the team. I started to black out several times during practice because one of the problems associated with albinism is not being able to tolerate the light and the heat. Living in Arizona was not a great combination for the two.

My coach was also my math teacher. He even split up me and my best friend in class as a consequence. Why were people so mad at things I couldn't control? My confidence started shrinking. I cut my losses and decided to try out for the basketball team. I made that too, but my cousin didn't. She spent hours practicing after school. She had such passion. I felt guilty and bad for her. So I quit. She was added to the team, I was happy about that, but most of my friends were on the team too, so I had to find new friends since they felt like I pretty much abandoned the team. I stopped playing basketball.

You know those definitive moments that sometimes change everything? Shatter a perception or change your reality? I've had a few of those. When I was 15 and preparing to get my driver's permit, (I was really determined to get my license at age 16), I was driving in the Walmart parking lot with my dad. It was all good, and I thought I was doing a great job, I went to park and I hit the curb.

I remember the scene perfectly. It was right across from Taco Bell and we were on the far end of the parking lot where it was completely empty. I went to park and I turned into a spot next to the curbing. Why I chose that spot, I don't know, but all I heard was a scraping noise and felt a thump. Whoops, I had just hit the curb. I was about to laugh about it until I saw the expression on my dad's face. He was just shaking his head. He told me something I can still hear clear as day, crisp as air.

My smile turned into a trembling frown, "Missy, when are you going to give it up and realize maybe you shouldn't be driving? You don't have depth perception. Maybe you shouldn't try so hard and just accept that you have limitations." Ouch. That one hurt.

My almost smile turned to a quivering frown. Although there was no damage to the truck, there was a definite impact, like a sucker punch to my soul. So I did just that. I went home and threw my permit away. That was a decisive moment for me. Almost like the physical act of throwing that one hope in the trash, throw away all of them, along with my dreams and aspirations.

Things started changing. I allowed myself to become defeated. I started to become a people pleaser. I left my school and my friends to go to a new school, a charter school that allowed me to take college classes and graduate early from high school. I was all on top of that.

The only thing I wanted to do was get away from my house, especially from my dad. It would take a whole book to write my experiences from my teenage years, but in a nut shell, I had some traumatizing experiences that left me completely disempowered. Traumas I let affect my whole life.

It took me years to finally admit those events, and it wasn't until I was brought into a sheriff's office a few years later that I felt safe enough to admit that yes, I had indeed been raped at 15. They were trying to convict the guy and someone who suspected I too may have been a victim had tipped them off. That had taken place three years earlier. I hadn't talked about it until then.

Anyhow, since that experience at age 15, I continued to make poorer and poorer decisions. I graduated early from high school at 17, moved out, shacked up with my boyfriend whom my parents hated, and dropped out of college.

Another definitive moment. I was sitting in my parent's front yard under the big tree my siblings and I used to hang and plop down from onto the trampoline. I had invited two guys over. Both were in love with me. In fact, they were best friends. One was my fiancé, the other, a close family friend. My dad came up to me, sat down next to me under my childhood tree and told me that I needed to make a decision. I needed to make up my mind. I needed to choose one of them and move on with my life.

I broke up with my love and fiancé because I didn't know what I wanted. Actually, I did, but it wasn't what my family wanted. So I threw it away. (Do you see the pattern?) Instead, I married someone I thought my parents would be happy with, particularly my dad. I thought he would give me a better life and that everyone would be happy. Everyone was, except me.

We had been married a year, the year of HELL, and then decided to get a divorce. We actually tried to get an annulment since we didn't have kids, but they didn't let us. Anyhow, I was so excited to move on with my life. So was he.

Then we found out I was pregnant. My mind was blown. I was on the Depo Provera shot. This was not supposed to happen. I had not even thought about having kids at that point and here I was about to be a mom and I was a mess. I was still a lost little girl. We got remarried; I got cleaned up and took my mom role seriously.

Six years and three kids later, I was sitting on the train tracks in my car, debating whether or not to get out of the way of the oncoming train. (I did end up getting my license at 18 after being pulled over without insurance, registration or a license and I had to get my license to get out of the ticket).

Definitive moment. How did I let my life get here? My marriage was hell. The only thing I was living for was my kids. My life sucked. I was going back to my addictions. I was making choices that made staying in my marriage difficult. I asked myself the question...*Why are you doing this? This isn't me.* Then it hit me. I was living my life for everyone else. I was a people-pleaser. I had let all my dreams go so I could live my life for the sake of other people's happiness! I was paying a high price for this.

Suddenly, I knew what I needed to do. I needed to start making new choices. Empowering choices. My first step was standing up for myself and getting a divorce. Was it hard? Yes. Was it worth it? Absolutely. I started letting go of the fear and the doubt that had held me back since that day in the parking lot when I hit the curb, and I threw my dreams and aspirations away.

That voice I had shut out spoke back up. The pull I experienced long ago became stronger. The call became unignorable. I took my life back. I let go of the need to be liked. I reclaimed my life and my calling. I married a man who is my Prince Charming. We had two kids together.

Today, my life is full. I have purpose. My ex and I are good friends. His wife and I are best friends. I am eager once again to make my mark in this world. I am doing it. I speak with hundreds of highly successful people every year. I hold events that make a difference. I own my own company where I help other moms find purpose and meaning, and honor that call to make a difference in the world while honoring their biggest role as a mother.

It's what I'm here to do. I stopped seeing through the eyes of limitation and fear. I took my obstacles and made them my opportunities. The eyes I see through now are the eyes of intuition, the eyes of seeing the big picture. The eyes of seeing people's blocks, limited beliefs, and the root of what holds them back.

My legal blindness helps me assist people in finding their light so they can shine in all of their brilliant light. How? I'm able to "see" under the surface and through the patterns, false beliefs and thinking that keep women from living their highest potential. I help them get past those blocks and anchor in the thinking that will take them to their dreams, and give them actionable plans to actually achieve their life and business goals.

Being legally blind was never a limitation; it only was when I bought into that idea.

We all have a calling as moms and women. Are you living up to yours?? If not, I am on a mission to take you to the other side so you can live a life you love and leave a legacy of success. It's beautiful, freeing, and empowering.

One of the favorite aspects in my business is taking mothers to six-figure incomes. It's easy when you are on purpose and connected.

You can only change the world by changing your world. You can only grow your dreams as big as you grow your life. If you're a mother and want to ignite your life with success check, out my website www.melissaleblanc.com and grab my free gift: "The Busy Mom's Productivity Toolkit."

Hit your goals in half the time; the ultimate resource to take back your time so you can take back your life. Here are some tips from my blog:

1. ***Get comfortable being uncomfortable.*** If you're sitting in your comfort zone, you're not growing and you're not moving toward success.

2. ***Schedule business and family around you, not everybody else.***

3. ***Celebrate.*** Celebrate your little wins and big successes. Otherwise, you'll always be chasing the next thing without ever feeling successful.

4. ***Be intentional.*** Know the "why" behind what you are doing . Otherwise it's easy to lose your passion, give up and get distracted.

5. ***Develop a strong mindset.*** Your mind must be strong enough to support you and take you to your goals and dreams.

6. ***Work with others who believe in you and your vision of success.*** Mentor with those who are where you want to be.

Gillian Manuela

Gillian Manuela is an author, angel reader, intuitive animal communicator, energy intuitive and healer. She works with clients holistically to assist them in balancing their field energetically. Her work with people allows them to open up to the joy, peace and love residing within them. Gillian works with Ascended Masters and Angels and channels Goddess Isis. She is a clear communicator from higher realms to help those on their path in their highest good.

Contact Information:
Website: www.gillianmanuela.com
Email: Gillian@gillianmanuela.com

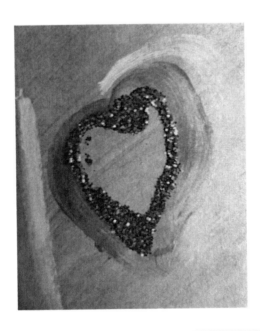

There Must Be More

By Gillian Manuela

s I sit with George, my tree in the sunshine, I wonder what to write because my life is full of ups and downs. I really thought that I lived a generally mundane life. But when you start to break it down, it has not been mundane at all; it is that you forget the bad times and even the good times.

My crisis point hit about ten years ago when I felt that there really must be more to life than just being born, working and then dying. What was the point of that? That was when it started to awaken me to the fact there was more to this than first meets the eye.

So my story starts about ten years ago and it has been slow, painfully slow, to the point of frustration at times. I know you should not compare yourself to others but it always creeps in. I have found myself questioning why others find it so easy to find their solution, to get connection to know where they are going. The problem is that the frustration seems to just block the way and stops me from moving forwards.

I have grasped every little thing that I have been told by healers, energy healers, and others and use their ideas to make myself feel better at the time, but over time, I find that it does not work for me any longer and forget to continue with it. Don't get me wrong—I have had some fabulous healers over the time which I have felt at the time was useful to me and buoyed me up so I would say that it was part of my journey to enlightenment. But with me, if something does not work instantly, I lose interest, a short attention span I suppose.

In 2009, our gorgeous dog passed over the Rainbow Bridge. We had to assist her in passing as she was in so much pain and struggling as her organs were starting to close down. My guides have said that the Rainbow Bridge is a path of least resistance for the transgressing animal. "Rainbow Bridge" is a phrase we have coined to help us understand and accept the concept of animals dying.

Just after her passing, within the hour, I felt a strange sensation on my face across the top of my cheek bones on both sides; it was like something pressing down on there. It would not go away, try as I might. This sensation stayed with me for many months. I was told that it was Jodie, our old dog, that was lying across my face. I feel she came back to assist me in moving forward, to find out why there was this sensation and so my adventure started.

I can remember one of my first healings using prayer. It was so surreal! I do not want to say who it was in case it offends but whilst they recited the channeled prayer for my healing, all I could think was "what the hell is this?" I really had to stop myself laughing out loud and saying, "No way! How can this prayer, these words, help me?"

Although I had this experience, something made me go back and have more sessions. If these helped me, I cannot say, but on reflection, it was the beginning of the journey, the beginning of finding who I was.

Over the years, I have been to many healers and have also attended many different classes, but something had still to open up. I seem to be a tough nut to crack.

I think that I am connected to my guides but not in the way I would like. I want to have the voice that booms out at me and gives me the information. I do need to be more content with what I have achieved. I know now that I do feel energy, especially when I stop and feel inside of me. I feel this rushing of tingles through my body.

By being quiet and just observing how you feel within yourself, you too could experience this as well. If you just sit and focus on your breath and then allow a white light to come down from above you and light up all of your chakras as the light flows down through your body, from the crown to the root chakra at the base of your spine. Then allow the light to flow down into the Earth from the root chakra and the soles of your feet, down into the center of the Earth, so that you feel grounded.

Once this is done, breathe gently and feel around your body to see how you feel, any tingles, aches, pains, or other sensations. Then guide the loving light into the areas of pain. This short meditation will help guide you to start to feel the energy within yourself.

I used to be emotionless. I felt like a block of wood unable to feel anything. I felt that all emotions had been sucked out of me. I was an empty shell or that was what I thought. I think I used to stuff my emotions down so that I would not hurt when I was younger. As a child and young adult, I was always fearful and afraid of asking for things from my parents. I always felt they disapproved of me and they seemed to shout at me. I don't think they meant to control me like that, but I feel they knew no better themselves.

My story starts when I was little, before I was four years old, when I did not speak. I just used to point and my parents understood what I wanted at that moment. I think that I did not feel that it was important to speak because I got all that I wanted. I believe that I came into this world as a telepathic being, not needing to talk. The only ones who were important were my guides on the other side, they were my friends, and they kept me company. I did not need the things in this world. This world was alien to me and frightened me. There were several times when I used to try to escape from my parents, going on adventures.

When I was 18 months old, we moved into a new house, I disappeared off through all of the gardens and then another time, I tried to squeeze under the garden gate, which was not successful as I got stuck.

At four years old, I went to nursery school and it was then that not talking was starting to cause a problem so I decided to start to talk but in doing so I decided to stop talking to my guides as much. Talking was very difficult for me as I could not get my tongue around some of the words. I could not translate the sound in my head to my tongue and then out as a sound. It can be still difficult even now.

So my next stage of life started. I was starting to talk and go to school. The first few months of school were awful. The weather was very bad, the snow was deep and my mum could not come and collect me from school at lunchtime because she could not push the pram through the snow easily. So I had to stay for school lunches. I hated the school lunches and got force fed near enough every day by the lunch ladies towards the end of the lunch break. It was not a good experience that I would recommend for any child. For some reason and it still sticks in my mind, they would not allow me to eat a banana that I took into school so it would stay in my bag for days until it got over ripe.

I was a good little helper at school. I liked to feel useful even at this tender age and as my father had spent an afternoon teaching me how to tie shoe laces using his leg as my prop, I put it to good use. I would help the teacher get all my class mates ready for going home, tying shoe laces and helping put on coats. My mother could not work out why I was always late out until she asked my teacher and so my quest started to be helpful to others.

At school, I had few friends and did not hang around with many outside of school. This happened to me throughout school; I would just have a friend or two and would see them only occasionally outside of school. I always felt that I did not fit in, they would say things and I would get the wrong idea of what they were saying. I don't know if it was because I was not streetwise or that my parents were quite controlling, as I was not allowed to go many places. My mother in particular was not happy for me to be out much.

I use to have great conversations with myself and in fact still do to this day. It is especially good when I feel upset, talking to myself always seems to calm me and I can solve problems whilst I talk, just thinking the problem in the head quietly just does not work for me. Speaking it out, out loud really does help to bring the problem to life and to get solved. Maybe I am talking to my guides and they are giving me the answers as a channel through me or maybe my words are calming and healing me without my realizing. It is one way of releasing any pressure or stress that can build up if you do not vent it out. It is better to let go than to hold it in and then cause dis-ease in the body.

In my mid-twenties, I went through a crisis of not being able to travel to work. I used to work in London; it was an hour ride on the train every morning and evening. One day, out of the blue, I had a panic attack or fear attack and could not get out of the car to go into the train station to get the train. I had to ask my husband to drive me back home.

At the time, I also was very tired all of the time, doing just the smallest thing used to exhaust me. I used to wake up in the morning between 5am and 6am with my stomach churning and feeling sick and scared. In the end, I went to see a doctor and he prescribed some tranquillizers that helped me to overcome the fear of the train journey.

It was also strange that after this I could not read horror books, like I used to. The horror books just seemed to make the problem worse. I was always happiest if I could travel with someone, sometimes I would go to the other side of London just so I could travel with my sister. I eventually stopped taking the tranquilizers and started to be able to travel to work with not too many prob-lems. Although the fear would raise its head every so often, I managed to cope with it better.

There are several ways I have learnt to cope with my anxiety now:

- Deep breathing and letting go of all stresses in the body on the out breath, visualizing the stress leaving in a black or grey cloud. This is especially good if there is an emotional knot in the body.

- Tapping on the K29 points, which are one inch below the collar bone and about one inch from the end of the collar bone. I find this very relaxing and calming.

- Standing back from the situation that is causing the anxiety, looking at it with no emotion for it and so giving it no power to upset.

- Another way which is one of my favorites is to visualize tiny bombs in my mind and then blow them up with glitter dust falling all around. This helps to stop the problem rolling around your mind and eating into you.

Life just continued on this mundane hamster wheel—work and sleep—until I had my daughter. Life changed then. There was someone else around to look after.

Soon after my daughter was born, I found that I had cervical cancer, I had a smear test whilst I was pregnant that came back as unusual and six months after I had my daughter, I had to have another smear test. This was followed up by a visit for a hysteroscopy (camera) to see how bad it was. I can remember the doctor carrying out the hysteroscopy, saying to me it is not cancer but to me it did look bad.

Circumstances stopped me from having a biopsy for three months and when the results came back, I had DIN 3 cervical cancer and was told that I had to have an extended hysterectomy. This means that my ovaries had to be removed as well.

The couple of weeks leading up to the operation were awful. There were many tears. My main gripe was that I could not have any more children and I had wanted at least two but obviously the Universe had other ideas for me.

My surgeon was very concerned that the cancer had spread to the lymph nodes. He was so concerned that I had my operation within a couple of weeks. A few days after the operation, he joyfully came up to see me on the ward and presented me with a letter with the results of the test on my lymph nodes. My lymph nodes were clear of cancer. I still undertook radiotherapy even though it made me feel tired and very ill towards the end of the five weeks, just in case there was any cancer still present in the body. Maybe if it had happened now, I would have done things differently.

When my daughter was three years old, she ended up in hospital with some sort of fever, we never found out what it was. They treated this fever with aspirin, which at the time, I did not know was extremely bad for her. There was a family reaction to aspirin that I did not know about. She ended up having a seizure one week later because of low sodium and potassium salts in her body, just as we were about to be sent home for the weekend. We then had two weeks in hospital on tenterhooks because the doctors really did not know how to treat her. Some days, she looked like she was about to have another seizure because they were treating her with another derivative of aspirin.

Eventually the doctors sent her home depressed and unable to move without pain. She had lost weight and muscle and could not even walk. They had sent her home with an anti-inflammatory and a few days later whilst having a daytime nap, she jumped in her sleep, a reminder of the day she had her first seizure.

Why had this happened? I decided to look into what was in the anti-inflammatory that they sent her home with. I found that this anti-inflammatory contained aspirin or some derivative of aspirin. We stopped giving her the anti-inflammatory straight away.

I think this was my wake-up call to looking at how to be well and keep well in a more natural way, that pharmaceutical drugs are not the answer to everything.

When my daughter was five years old she started with eczema and instead of going to the doctors, I actually searched for a homeopath. I managed to find a homeopath in the nearest town. He would listen to the problems and then make up a remedy that had to be taken at certain times of the day. It always surprised me when she became ill during the course of the remedy and I would ring him and he would always know that she would be experiencing that problem at that time, during that stage. Even more surprising was that I had to speed up giving the remedy and by the end of the day, my daughter would be feeling better.

Life continued as everyone else's does, working, eating and sleeping with time at the weekends to be with the family.

In my mid-forties, I started to want to do something else. Life did not feel right. I started to trade stocks, but even with training, I did not have the right qualities to be able to stick out trades that were losing or even to pick the right trades. Apparently, that was not the way I was supposed to go; it was not my path.

I then decided to try and do my own online business and found some mentors to help me. When I had to decide what I wanted to do the business in, what were my passions, I seemed to be drawn to health, weight loss and women's health. I could never get these businesses off the ground. I don't know if there were blocks in me or even fears that stopped me from actually having a successful business. It was whilst searching for information for articles for my website that I discovered energy healing and that we have life purposes.

What was my life purpose? Why am I here? These were the questions I had. There had to be more to life. We do not just come to Earth to eat, work, sleep and die. It seemed too strange to think that was all there was. There had to be more. When we die, do we go for good? How can that be? There were so many questions.

So this led me to start looking around. I don't remember how I found the people I worked with. They seemed to have just appeared when maybe the time was right for me. It made me feel good when I spoke to these healers; it gave me the next piece in the puzzle—this great big puzzle with so many pieces missing.

Life is so like a jigsaw where we have to find the pieces to make the picture. Finding the pieces is not easy for many people; you have to look at what draws you, what interests you. For me, it was that so many people around me seemed to be in pain and ill that it seemed that the Universe was telling me that I am healer.

Looking back now I realize that the Universe must have been shouting at me to wake me to who I really am, but like so many other people, I was oblivious to the fact that there is a reason to us being here on Earth.

As you awaken, you gradually realize the big reason to being here and what part you are to play within the universe. We all come with different reasons to be here, but unfortunately, we forget when we are born and so we have to learn what it is. Many people will not find or even realize that there is a plan for each of us and that their lives could have been so different.

My life is still evolving and will do so until I die, I am sure. I have learnt and taken many healing modalities so far, including Reiki up to Reiki Master, EFT, and dowsing, to name just a few. As I write here, I am taking an animal communication and healing course that will help me to be able to help the animals in this world as well. Animals have problems just the same as us humans; sometimes their problems are not their own, but those of their human companions that they live with.

I am also able to read Angel cards and give readings in this way. It is strange how cards organize themselves to come out of the pack in the correct way and order that is right for the person. I do not look to predict the future, but give readings that will maybe provide some clarity on a situation or a healing if that is required.

Throughout my life, especially these last few years, I have been guided to do things that really interest me and that I enjoy to do. All of the courses that I have taken have been leading me along the pathway to way I am today. It is really important to enjoy what you do, to follow your passion.

Peace

We come and go
Always busy, never giving time to rest
Why not take a moment of your day
To rest and notice all around you
Notice the sweetness of the Earth
Notice the Nature that you pass each day
But do not see
Notice the calm that is present
The calm that is always there
But you do not see
Take this time to calm yourself
Calm yourself and to be at peace
And then you can go back to being busy
But that calm will seep through you
It will seep all through the day
Enjoy the calm and peace

Trust

Everyone lives from their beliefs
Which is not the best way to be
Your beliefs have been imposed on you
They are not even yours
Let go the beliefs and start to trust
Trust your inner self
Your inner self does not work with beliefs
Your inner self is caring and compassionate
Trust that little voice
That calls when you are in danger
Trust that gut feeling
When things do not feel right
Trust yourself that you are right
Trust yourself

Yan Yamamoto Ouadfel

Yan (Diane) Yamamoto Ouadfel, owner of Yan's Rainbow Essence, loves to play in and create from nature her healing gem sprays. Trained originally as a pharmacist, Yan began to evolve in her own life and discovery process by taking a special interest in the study of medicinal plants. For as long as she can remember, Yan "knew" that a world existed which followed the healing potential through the natural world, she just had to find it. Eventually, through her curiosity and passion along the way, it found her, and steadily placed her on her own path to healing and self-love.

Yan is an advanced crystal healer graduate from The Crystal Academy with Katrina Raphaell, and a certified Vibrational Healer, and guest teacher with Joy Gardner of the RMA Mystery School. Yan is currently completing her Homeopathic Practitioner Program from the American Medical College of Homeopathy @ PIHMA, in Phoenix, AZ. She also studies with homeopaths Ambika Wauters founder, and Vonette Thorner of Life Energy Medicine, is certified in sound healing qi-gong with Master Mingtong Gu, and will complete her Iridology training with Brenda Generali.

Yan plans to open a holistic private practice in 2017 for people and pets, to continue teaching, and to always strive to help raise human consciousness... She is a Libra.

Contact Information:
Email: yansrainbow@yahoo.com

Love's Evolving Resonance

By Yan Yamamoto Ouadfel

his moment could not have come any sooner, or any later, for that matter. This place that I hold within myself today had been waiting for me to arrive, for a very long time, even before I was born.

I never dreamed that 38 years ago, the contents of my existence would be turned over and dumped out. I was 12 years old, and I got called down to the school office. The teacher told me to leave my books on my desk, and go immediately to the principal's office. Someone was here to see me. The class became very silent, all eyes on me, as I quietly got up, following the direction from my teacher.

To my surprise, one of our neighbors was standing there in her jeans and sandals, nervously waiting for me. Confusion and shock came over me. I thought to myself, "Virginia's children were much younger and not in junior high so, why is she here, and what does this have to do with me?" The office lady told me to go with Virginia and we left in silence. As she drove, we took the route home.

I could feel the nervous upset coming from her, still with no talk, no explanation. The car ride home was going too fast, faster than the usual ten minutes from school to home. It was Indian Summer, as they used to describe early September in the Midwest, and the sun was shining, but the air was perfectly still. I don't even remember the birds singing. All was silent, only the sound of the car and Virginia's nervous breathing filled this gap.

As we pulled into the driveway, Virginia managed to whisper in a choked-up voice, holding back her tears, "Your mother needs you now, Honey," just as the car stopped, in perfect time with her words.

As I began to step out of the car, I felt a great departure come over me, and that I would never see Virginia again, or in the same way. I felt suddenly a sense of separation from everything. It was approximately 10:30 in the morning when I got picked up from school. I was 12 years old, almost three weeks away from my 13th birthday, starting my 8th grade year, on September 6, 1978, that I came home to find out that I lost my father to cancer.

Back then, the "Big C", as it was called, was often, and usually, a death sentence in itself, for so many people, as well as animals. Chemotherapy and radiation were still not refined, and not enough was known about cancer, from so many perspectives. Working-class people did not have luxuries to travel to exotic places that specialized in cancer management or life-saving treatments, if there could be any, and on that day, the big secret being kept from me was confirmed. The greatest fear I felt for my father was really true. He really did have cancer, and it took him.

Prior to my father's passing, my parents, who were loving and doing their best, decided to shield me from knowing that my father's predicament was the "Big C." Everything surrounding the "Big C" at that time, and for such a long time, was catastrophic, revolving around fear, doom, pain, and suffering for any family. Taking into consideration their understanding of my innate sensitivities, I look back now and recognize the magnitude of their love and compassion for me, a little, unassuming kid. I have no doubt that this decision was also a decision guided by Spirit. My parents' plight was also to be mine, energetically.

Dad developed pneumonia in the spring of that same year, and had a lingering cough that would not go away. By summertime, he began his own journey in and out of hospitals, attempting to try radiation, before he decided that the treatment was killing him faster than the disease itself, and elected to walk away from treatment to die in his own way.

Within four months, he began wasting, and ultimately, went down to 86 pounds before he took his last breath. I had a funny feeling and a silent fear, wondering if this is what cancer looks like.

At 12 years old, I tried to do my own research, listening to the news or reading about what cancer looks like. I still was not sure, and nobody talked to me about it. Dancing around full disclosure, my parents called it a cough, then a tumor. I was not completely clear . . . did tumor mean the same thing as cancer?

Eventually, my parents decided it was best that I no longer visit the hospital. This was one month before my father's passing. He was becoming unrecognizable through the ravages of cancer, and they felt the shock would be too great through my idealistic and sensitive lens, although I was somehow aware, that they were aware, that I could feel, even if I could not watch.

To reach out, I took a chance every morning and either jogged by or rode my bike past the hospital where Dad was. Up on one of the floors, where the stairwell climbed, was a large, picture window, and each morning, I would try to catch a glimpse of my father, standing in the window, wearing his blue robe. I recognized him in the distance by the shape of his person and from his blue robe, a Christmas gift from the year before.

When I saw him, I would stop and simply wave. I felt like a passing ship signaling to a beacon of light. The week before he passed, the beacon of light that was always standing in the window was not there to signal back to me. Perhaps in my hopeful and naïve denial, I feared and wondered if I had not gotten there in time and missed the schedule, although intuition told me otherwise.

Trying to be a good and obedient daughter in this time of crisis and upheaval, I did not press the "issue" or question. I felt I just simply needed to help take care of my mother and maintain myself and the household as best as I could, walking about by myself, through my own fears.

The following week, my lighted beacon returned to Spirit. My tiny, regular life changed completely. It felt like there was a huge explosion and as if I were a lone survivor standing among the wreckage.

Unbeknownst to me at that time, the illness that took my father, would also take my mother, but twenty years and one week later, in addition to other uncles on both sides of my family. Cancer was, and is, my inherent weakness, as well a teacher.

Being born into cancer inherently and energetically has brought me here, in this perfect moment of today. And while I have my ancestors to thank, I hope to gift back to my lineage the clearing of this weakness through the connections our bodies have with mind and spirit.

After being trained as a traditional pharmacist, with an interest and belief in medicinal plants, I have evolved and changed my life since. I am completing my homeopathic practitioner training, and along with other holistic, and bio-energetic modalities, such as Qi Gong, Sound and Color Healing, and other tools that work within the Laws of Nature, I will be able to help people and animals rebalance what is innately inherent in each and every one of us: the body's ability to return itself to balance and harmony for themselves and their lineage.

What does that mean really? It is about reconnecting You with the amazing God-given gift of your Vital Force. As one homeopath, Torako Yui, wrote so beautifully, "the reason for the body's loss of wisdom is a blockage in the flow of the vital force."

Boundaries and Boundless

The path to this and my path came out of many years of long, standing loss.

After Dad passed, my greatest fear, at the age of 12, was that I would lose my last parent, and especially to cancer. I prayed that Mom would be healthy and that she would be with me for a very long time, only to come face to face with this greatest fear when I was 32. It began when I was 29 years old.

My mother got diagnosed with colon cancer and went through a course of chemotherapy. I had already worked as a pharmacist, and was very hopeful that with a good oncologist, she would and could do very well. The thought of her dying was near, but as I watched her progress through the chemo, the good thoughts, prayers, healthier diet, and positive attitude, I tried to help by being there for her as much as I could, as a good daughter and companion through this crisis. She seemed to be defying the odds.

My mother, born in Japan, was a young girl when Hiroshima and Nagasaki were hit with the atomic bomb. Her family retreated to a cave in the mountains of Kobe for three days, following the atomic bomb on Nagasaki, and before the surrender of Japan during WII. She was quite a fiery person, strong-willed, and very engaged in life. I wondered if the effects of her childhood exposure to the atomic bomb could have set her up for what came as a surprise.

It was here, in coping with the possibility of Mom having cancer and my meeting my greatest fear, that I began my own healing journey into the realm of spirit healing, as well as bio-energetic medicine. Until that time, I did not really know or understand anything about the Holistic paradigm, as it truly is. I just knew, somehow, innately, that I needed to "shield" myself from what may be another bomb in my life. It felt like a natural step in my own right direction, the same way I feel a sense of "home" when I dig my hands through the soil and garden. For the first time, I felt I was pointing the compass of my life in what felt to be my true north.

I recall, at the age of 17, I finally tired of worrying about "what if" and cancer, and surrendered myself to nearly proclaiming to God, half angry, half in protest, "Ok, God, IF I am going to get cancer, I am not going to die from it. I am going to survive!"

Naïve and idealistic, this gave me the grit I needed to move on from the first bomb, pick myself up, and step away from fear. At the time, I could not have articulated this and was going by instinct. I had no idea I was stepping out of a place of fear. I was just summing up what was coming through. Where and how this thought even popped into my head could have been only guided by Spirit because I had no background to even conjugate a thought particle such as that.

It was something innate within my body's own ability to survive. I believe, on a longer-term protective level, my own body's vital force was speaking to me. This is when I began to listen to Spirit in ways I had never done before. Between the age of 12 and 17, I had angelic experiences, odd and blessed experiences, making my awareness more open to knowing that the veil between matter and spirit is attached, we are connected.

Later, during Mom's first bout with the colon cancer, I told her this story and created a mantra for her, that was inspired by what came through me at 17. Hers was customized to her. "I have cancer, but I am going to survive".

We created other mantras together during the times she received her chemotherapy treatments. In the beginning part of her treatment, she experienced terrible nausea, anticipatory anxiety, and stomatitis. Had I been further in my path of my current studies, I could have helped her with remedies, but what we had was faith and our mantras. I knew that one had to ask, without realizing this knowing. It was just there.

There was a mantra to shoo away the nausea, to think and command the nausea away, and to our happy delight, the mantras worked. We slowed down her chemotherapy drip rate, extending the time of infusion, and one day prior, Mom would begin her mantras. It worked! The combination of medication management, along with the visualization and mantras, allowed her to tolerate her chemotherapy treatments much better than when she started. She detached herself from a place of fear. No more nausea, no more anticipatory anxiety surrounding her treatments. She shifted herself and connected the mind and spirit to her body. It was there that I began to see, through example, the power of our minds, as well as the power of Spirit, and how this can help to govern our physical bodies.

That year, although my own foundation was crumbling and coming out from under my feet, I was trying to be a caretaker and the ideal daughter in a time of crisis. The caring caregiver put herself last. With my own foundation crumbling, I fell away from my own knowing of self-love, and of understanding that just being, existing is enough. That was not exercised within myself, and little did I know, the bombs were already exploding. I was too immersed to recognize what was within myself and what never got healed from the get go.

A year and a half later, Mom was diagnosed with a new cancer, an aggressive lung cancer. It was in the same area that my father had his cancer. How could this be? We thought Mom was in the clear and all was going well. All was going well and life got back to normal. Well, the old life that was now burdened with much unattended due to grief and stress.

Mom's immune system could not recover. This time, it was terminal. I remember the surgeon explaining to me that my mother was a walking time bomb. A tumor was pressing upon her heart and that she could go any minute. Maybe, if she is lucky, she will last one month, at best. Two months passed and she began to regain energy and seemed thrive. She went on to live an extra five months.

We worked with Mom as best as we could, mostly loving and supporting her, as she went directly from the hospital to hospice care. This was it; my old fears were coming to be. Before, we celebrated life, and her first cancer, and cancer itself, seemed like another life passed. I began in my own way to prepare for loss. I did not want to fall completely down and I teetered on a certain extent of denial while walking a tightrope of the fragility of life yet desiring freedom from structure, wanting to be boundless and free. And the survivor in me innately also began to step more deeply into my own spiritual and energetic healing.

During this time, I was living as a renegade, desiring to not abide by my own inner rules, wanting to feel adrenaline. It was a time of sky-diving and bungee-jumping, relationships with people who fostered abandoned wildness, who were unavailable emotionally or physically as true people for my highest and best interests of my life, while trying to be strong and hold it together for my mother and sister. The energy of cancer was so close to me that it began to manifest through my emotional self, my emotional body. I knew that soon I would be separated from all that I was enmeshed in as far as having parents.

It was a scary time and yet a beautiful time with Mom. My senses were heightened and I began to celebrate the little things, the moments. I cherished life differently, and felt the metamorphosis happening simultaneous to Mom's dying. Yet, as a parent knows their children, Mom knew that I was keeping too much inside and feeling great pain which I refused to express, at least in front of her.

I threw myself into places wanting comfort, but coming up empty. Eventually, in September, 20 years and one week after Dad passed, Mom joined him, on September 11th. And although I was out there in the world free, I also felt what it may feel like to be an orphan.

It was a time of my climb as well as my descent, all at the same time. Bound and boundless. I lost my foundation to reason, and lost myself to my place in this world. I did not need to ask my parents' permission or their opinions, but I did in Spirit. This sense of freedom felt very unusual to me.

Now stripped down, after having come through, I know this major life change was my greatest blessing. It was not until I lost materially (almost everything) that I got reminded that I was walking through gates and each challenge blessed me. I had to learn to let go and most importantly to trust. Lessons of trust pushed into my life and I had one foot in confusion and the other foot stepping onto the path of being my own spiritual warrior.

Along the way, I fortified myself spiritually, taking on energy of a spiritual warrior within myself. I needed to save myself; no one else was going to save me. This was between me and God.

My first step into a deeper self-exploration, where the rubber needed to meet the road, came through during my crystal healing training. My love for stones and nature stepped forward. Here is where I first really learned about "healer, heal thyself." I had to walk the walk. I studied and devoted myself spiritually.

As my spiritual explorations expanded, the people in my life who were not serving my best interest began to first become repelled and then fall away. I had been living within and among deception, hopeful in the wrong places, and that started to show itself. In the process, there was the financial crisis starting in 2008. Eventually, I lost most everything except myself. I stepped into my own healing, as the Divine timing would only have it, at the perfect time. It was also the support of a dear friend, Karen, a breast cancer survivor, who was my support and witness through it all.

All that was going to turn upside down did, yet I still plugged on. I felt more whole the more stripped down the life I knew and the chaos I created unfolded. As things were falling away, I was being lovingly carried away on the wings of Angelic forces, protecting me and blessing me along the way, with Karen's reassurances that "no, I was not crazy." I began to understand what was wrong on the outside is a reflection of something not healed or calling for healing on the inside, and having started the journey, I knew the only way out was to go inward and through.

Through many years of study and devotion, but mostly Love, I returned to a place of my essence, to a place of self-love and forgiveness. From the realm of the mineral kingdom came great healing and insight. Through daily breath meditations, prayer, energetic work, yoga, returning to the things within nature that I felt in communion with: shamanic work, toning with color and sound, Qi-Gong, and to homeopathy, my vital force led me back not just to balance, but prevented me from having a debilitating illness overtake me, and strengthened my immune system, provided me with clarity, and continues to help me clear the layers within that are ready to be healed, as well as the karmic layers and the karmic debt to be lovingly cleared.

In turn, people with cancer were finding me, through word of mouth, asking for assistance to help ease the discomfort they were experiencing through chemotherapy or radiation. I made tea blends from medicinal mushrooms and the clients did amazingly well as they went through their chemotherapy. I stuck to the foundations of researching the research I could find, and the rest was on a wing and a prayer with faith that the Divine Source was channeling through me. Karen believed in me, we believed, and the clients believed.

Later, after the dust was settling from the losses, I knew that it was time to make a commitment to changing my career and working in a field of bio-energetic healing. I chose homeopathy, as it was a natural fit. How exciting that all of its remedies come from nature- they are vital and alive. After starting my homeopathic training, I learned about resonance. I asked myself before, "Why had these people found me? Why me?" It was the resonance they felt, of how close cancer was to me. Now, I am clearing my hereditary weakness of cancer through homeopathy, and one of the remedies is a bio-energetic imprint of cancer itself. I would have never come to this had it not been for All.

To recognize that I was carrying this energy, and to need this remedy to help clear my genetic predisposition to cancer, I experienced great losses of many kinds and sustained the heartache over a long period of time. I experienced deep grief that never grieved fully, until I began to do my work. Heartbreak and heartache. I experienced letting go of the need for perfection and forgave myself for being human, for being just the regular girl. I released all that was not mine and thanked all that came through, yet fell away.

What came after was love in my life, a beautiful marriage, a new career that is in alignment with my life's purpose, a renewal, a bigger connection to All that Is and within the new paradigms, miracles, the Divine Feminine, and the ability to share part of my story, which has lead me to my own healing, so that others may hopefully be inspired or benefit. Thanking God every day, the Archangels, my ancestors, spirit guides and guides, guardians, the mineral, plant, and animal kingdoms, I began to understand that my circumstance was a pre-destined layer that needed to be healed through experience and walking through. Always grateful, even with the losses, I never felt alone.

What encompasses health? As I stand here today, I can say that it is the integration of our Whole Being: spirit, mind and body. Forgiveness and gratitude are huge keys that I have found help to keep the doors of possibility and health open. Universal Life Force is plentiful, it is abundant and always there. We just have to bring it into our Being, as much as we can. Recognizing the challenges our ancestors have faced with their health gives us the opportunity to heal our lineage as well as ourselves, those around us, and the planet by waking up the memory of what we previously knew before, of body, mind, spirit connection.

The Laws of Nature guide us. If there are two frequencies, the lower frequency will always adjust to the higher frequency, and our bodies already know this. It just needs the right tools to accomplish this. Now, as I sit on a plane that is ready to turn onto the runway of my next deeper journey, I remember my father, the beacon of light, and I wave from my heart. Thank you, for shielding me, so that I may come into my own, and for being one of my greatest teachers and gifts of this lifetime. Thank you, dear Dad.

Gina M. Pirone

Gina Pirone has been very sensitive all of her life. She is a gifted Psychic Intuitive and has the ability to connect with animals as well as people. Many people recognize Gina as an Intuitive Animal Communicator. She is guided by the Divine, her Guides, Higher Self and her Angels and receives the messages crystal clear. Her gifts of sensing, feeling and knowing are always correct. She receives the answers as it comes to her and she tells it like it is. Also, Gina is the Owner and CEO of Hear From Your Pets, LLC.

Gina is an Indigo Child, Author, Healer, Certified Angel Card Reader and a Reiki Master. She is very passionate about helping people and their pets get along and be happy. Gina has helped many people find solutions to their situation of what's going on with their pet. Receive your Free Gift—"Five Things That Your Animals Want You To Know"—at www.ginapirone.com

Contact Information:

Website: www.GinaPirone.com
Email: gina@ginapirone.com

My Enlightened Life

By Gina M. Pirone

One day as I was waiting to see the doctor for my annual exam, I was thinking back to how things have unfolded in my life. I was under such an incredible amount of pressure and anxiety that I just couldn't breathe. It felt as though I were suffocating. I was handling a great deal at that time. When the doctor came in, she took one look at me and I burst into tears. She sat with me and spoke to me about depression, which I didn't know much about at that time. I asked her how I could be depressed. I didn't know anyone that was depressed or at least that's what I thought.

After the exam, as I sat in my car thinking about what the doctor had said to me, I couldn't stop crying. I was suffering from depression. I didn't know the depth of the depression, only that I was crying, felt so sad, lonely and helpless all the time. I felt that no one would miss me if I were gone.

Let me tell you about myself. I was born in Yonkers, New York in 1960 and lived in the Bronx until I was eight. I enjoyed playing hopscotch, jumping rope and going on the swings. I used to have a lemonade stand on the corner where people would come and go to the subway and I enjoyed going to the corner store for chocolate egg creams.

My father left us when I was two, my brother, Tom, was four and my sister, Ann, was just born. We did see our father on Saturdays, only when he decided to show up. My brother and I would wait for him sitting on the curb; our mother felt our pain of him not showing up. I know my brother was very upset and I would go into my room and stay there and cry.

Looking back, I remember seeing my mother with bars on her legs to walk. She didn't have the will to live anymore. It wasn't until our grandparents brought us to the hospital to see her, to show her what she has to live for, her children, that she improved. We had given her the will to live and get stronger again. During that time of my mother's recovery, my grandparents, my father's parents, had taken care of us. We were very close to them and they knew their son hadn't done the right thing.

When I was older and looked back at my mother's heartbreak of grief and her falling apart after my father had left, it showed me she had not been taught or given any tools by her parents or family on how to cope with this type of loss, which seemed like depression or maybe it was prolonged sadness and grief that she hadn't processed. She was the first one in her family to have to deal with this and she was alone.

I cried and thought I was to blame for my father's leaving. I missed him terribly and suffered by not having him in my life. I shut down and blocked out everyone and everything. I always had a love for animals and knew at a young age, I had a special connection with them. I could feel if they were happy or sad, wanted to play or nap, if they didn't feel well or just wanted to be left alone.

Over the years, we had cats, hamsters, rabbits, fish, dogs and a guinea pig to mention a few. I would always talk to them and show them love. Also, during this time of sadness and disbelief, I would play and talk with my dolls and stuffed animals. I used to see white sparkles, which at the time I didn't know what they were. Years later, I had found out that the white sparkles I was seeing were fairies. I have always noticed their presence and protection. I didn't remember this until recently because I was so shut down.

Those years without my father in my life taught me to heal myself from my heart. By forgiving him for leaving, I was sending him love as I was healing myself during this time. It has opened up my heart, which is filled with so much love. I became more confident learning about love, loss and forgiveness. I would not be the woman I am today without learning these lessons. They gave me a special love of animals that I have never felt before. My father has since passed but I want to thank him for bringing me closer to animals and how much love I have in my heart to heal others.

When I was eight, my mother remarried and we moved to New Jersey. I had a stepfather and two stepbrothers, Rich and Larry, who I call my brothers. We all got along and had the usual fights and disagreements siblings have. We were all treated the same.

It was unfortunate that my stepfather screamed and yelled all the time; this made me stutter. He complained about everything and always told us how stupid we were and would never amount to anything. I couldn't take any more of his mental abuse so I moved out when I was 19 years old. He has since passed away.

What I realize from the way he treated me, is that it is important to be patient, considerate of other people and their feelings, listen to what someone has to say, to not interrupt them when they are speaking and to show respect to every person and animal.

I graduated Irvington High School in 1978. During that time, I was Class President for three years and Captain of the Flag Swingers. When I graduated, I didn't want to go to college. I decided to go to Katharine Gibbs, which is a well-established secretarial school in

New Jersey and in New York. After graduating with high honors, I was excited to begin my life, get married and have a family.

The man I had been dating for six years and planned on marrying had other plans and they weren't with me. I was heart-broken and loved him very much. As they say, things happen for the best. I was very sad for quite some time. He has taught me about forgiveness. It is one of the hardest things to do, but I have forgiven him and hope that he is happy and well.

A few years went by and I did meet and fall in love with Joe. We dated for two years and in September of 1990, we got married. I was 30 years old at the time. Let me tell you about Joe. He is the most loving, caring, considerate, honest and smartest man I have ever met. He has the greatest sense of humor and he always makes me laugh, even after all these years.

As time went by, we tried to have children and nothing worked. We tried for a few years then decided to see a specialist. Following the advice of the specialist during the procedure, he impregnated me with five embryos to see if any of them would take. I was so happy and excited to finally start the family I had dreamed of since I was a little girl. I was looking at the tiny baby clothes, picturing what they would look like on and just couldn't wait to hold him or her in my arms. When I went back to the doctor for my checkup, he told us that I wasn't pregnant. They all had terminated and I couldn't believe not even one survived.

This sent me back into a depression. I was very sad, angry and couldn't understand why I wasn't able to have children. It was impossible for me to go to baby showers, christenings or anything else to do with babies at that time. I felt that I was being punished for something.

Again, I called upon my spirit guides, angels and the Divine to guide me to go within my heart and forgive with my heart to heal my pain. This time it took me quite some time to release the anger, blame and forgiveness, but I had faith that God would take care of me. I know he had a reason.

One day in June of 1996, we went to a family picnic and all of a sudden I felt lightheaded and had cramps. I knew it couldn't be my period because I had it two weeks earlier. I ignored how I was feeling and just thought it might have been the weather, since it was very hot outside. I went into the house to use the bathroom, and all I can say is, thank God I did. The blood went through everything I was wearing and we left the picnic to go home.

All that night, I was bleeding and going to the bathroom. We called my OB/GYN to let him know what was going on and he said to keep an eye on it and keep in touch with him, thinking it would slow down, but it didn't. All I remember was coming out of the bathroom and collapsing onto the bed. Joe jumped up and called 911 and my OB/GYN. He said to meet him at Monmouth Medical Center in New Jersey.

I don't remember when the paramedics got there. I told them I could walk down the stairs, which was impossible because I couldn't even stand up. I didn't even comb my hair. It was serious. Joe told me later on that they were asking me questions and I was giving them bizarre answers. I didn't know what year it was; who was the President; and what month it was. I didn't remember them asking me anything. I was feeling so tired and kept hearing the siren, thinking to myself, *is that really necessary?*

When we reached the hospital emergency entrance, the doctor in charge called in their full-time nurses (my angels) to take care of me. I thought to myself, wow that was really nice of him, not realizing that my condition was very serious. I remember lying on a gurney with my head tilted all the way down so that the blood could go to my head. I heard Joe call my parents and tell them to get down there right away.

While I was lying there fading in and out, I did have a near-death experience. My heart stopped for a minute or two. It was very peaceful as I was thinking about my family and how much I loved them. I was feeling so much love and everything was white. I saw a small white light far off in the distance, and as it came closer, it got bigger and bigger until I saw all white. Everything was so beautiful and serene. The hospital staff was giving me blood transfusions until I was stable enough to go to a room.

Joe had stayed with me all day and night, making sure I was getting the correct blood type. Later that evening, the doctor from the emergency room came into my room and put his hand on my knee. He said to me, "You are one strong young lady. God must have special plans for you."

It wasn't until then that I realized I had died. My blood count was down to 4. That's why I felt very calm and everything was white and surreal to me. All I felt was love, but as you can see, I made it through.

In 1998, my mother Virginia needed heart surgery and I became her caretaker from that point forward. She lived with me, Joe, and our two cats, Max and Sophie. I was taking her to physical therapy three times a week for several months to get her strong again. She enjoyed knitting, going to the movies, loved the beach, shopping and going out to eat with the family.

My mother was diagnosed with Parkinson Syndrome in 2000. I believe it was caused when she lost her balance and missed the handrail. She fell down a flight of stairs, hitting her head very hard against the wall. Life tremendously changed for all of us after her accident.

We spent every day together from morning until night. We would laugh about something every day. One day she asked me to change her shoes in the box she was going to be laid out in. I asked her why. She told me that the shoes she had on were much more comfortable. We looked at each other and laughed. She saw my eyes tearing up and I told her how much I loved her and how much I was going to miss her.

A few nights later, as I was tucking her into bed, I noticed she was looking over my shoulder at something. I felt she saw her family behind me, but she didn't want to talk about it. She wanted to thank me for being a wonderful daughter and that she loved me, and I told her she was a wonderful mother and that I loved her very much, too. It was a very emotional time for both of us. I had given her a bell to ring at night if she needed me. She was always thanking me for taking care of her and I told her that I wouldn't hesitate to do it again.

I had hospice coming in to check on her. I remember so clearly what my mother had said to me. "My time is coming soon." It was very difficult for her to eat, walk and talk. What is living life if you couldn't enjoy the things that you love? As the family was gathering around her bed to say how much they loved her and how much she would be missed, I whispered in her ear, "It's okay to let go now."

Shortly after that, she took her last breath. To this day, I sometimes hear the bell ring and I know she's letting me know everything is okay. She was a very loving mother, had patience and was always there for me.

In June of 2006. I decided to have a full hysterectomy due to the problems I had over the years with endometriosis and fibroid tumors. It was very painful every month and I knew I had to do something about it. As I look back, it was the best decision for me to make.

My spiritual journey began after my mother passed away on March 6, 2005. I read books, listened to many spiritual speakers and teachers, went to seminars and expos. I learned so much about myself. I was happy to begin my life, which I know had to do with being a healer.

I learned how to meditate and would raise my vibration so high that I have heard the Angel's Choir singing. It was the most beautiful music I have ever heard. One time, I saw a portal. Both sides were blurred and the middle was crystal clear. Another time when I closed my eyes, everything was orange. I then saw Archangel Michael swinging his sword, down to the left then down and up to the right as he was jumping from side to side, like he was dueling with someone. He turned and looked at me, smiled and continued jumping back and forth swinging his sword. He looked like he was having fun.

I remember during my Reiki class when I was meditating, I saw an angel. In my mind, I told her to come closer, that she was too far away. Soon after that class, I felt a need to make a fairy garden. I didn't know why or how to even make one. I went to a garden center, bought a big planter, soil, miniature trees and flowers and other items I needed to make one. I went home and put everything together. I ended up making two. The other one was a big cup and saucer planter, which tipped over and broke during a storm.

After I made these fairy gardens, I had no desire to make any more. The following week, my teacher told me that I was seeing fairies and that they were only two inches high. Little did I know that the fairies were nudging me to make them a fairy garden. I've included a picture of my fairy garden to show you. Soon after, I became a Reiki Master.

My fairy gardens

I have always been very intuitive and sensitive my whole life. When I watched a movie, I was able to figure out what was going to happen next. My gifts were starting to open more and more as time went on. My gifts of sensing, knowing and feeling are getting stronger each day.

I have always had long conversations with God. To me, he is "I AM THAT I AM." Some people don't understand what a spiritual path is. You would definitely know what it is if you were on one.

When I started out on this beautiful journey of awakening, I wasn't sure where it would take me. I am sure that I am a pure and clear channel for myself and other people. I always call in my Higher Self for validation on any situation that arises and I listen to my Divine Guidance for healing, wisdom and helping people and animals find love and joy in their lives.

I know that my spiritual journey hasn't ended here. I feel there will be many surprises along the way as they awaken in me. Life is so beautiful and precious, so enjoy every day as if it were your last.

I've learned so much from Anne Deidre and would like to thank you, Anne, for sharing your gifts of intuition and encouragement. You guided me to open up my gifts of being an Animal Intuitive, taking your Intuitive Life Coach Course and becoming a Certified Angel Card Reader. Also, you have helped me to grow spiritually and have given me the confidence to know that I can do anything in this world.

Although I have been through difficult challenges that have felt very depressing at times, I don't feel that I was chronically depressed but very sad, grieving and depressed at the situation and circumstances.

When my heart stopped beating, there was a rebirth inside of me. I no longer have those long depressive episodes and feel quite optimistic, hopeful and inspired about the possibilities with my intuition and being of service with others. I am so blessed to be feeling so much love, joy and gratitude every day.

While I was writing *My Enlightened Life*, my cat Sophie passed away on May 26, 2016 at the age of 14. She was such a special part of our family. She was born on September 11, 2001. She was my beautiful and precious little girl. I considered her my "daughter" and loved her with all my heart.

Sophie

I was heartbroken when I found out that she had been diagnosed with squamous cell carcinoma (mouth cancer) and there
wasn't any treatment for this type of fast-growing cancer, which I
didn't understand because she was always indoors. One day, I told
her to give me a sign to let me know when she was ready to go to
the vet for her final visit. Suddenly, she looked at me and tilted her
head up and it involuntarily started to shake, which I had never
seen her do before.

Max and Sophie

I knew that was the sign that she wanted me to see. I said to her, "Okay, Sophie, tomorrow is your day to go HOME," as the tears kept running down my face with the enormous pain I felt in my heart. I couldn't stop crying as I glanced at the empty pet carrier in the back seat. I was in such pain, grief and sadness to know that I would never see her again.

While she was ill, I felt that her soul wanted to leave her body. She would sit there and stare straight ahead, and even when I called her, she didn't hear me. It was as it she was in another world, which she was.

I know she needed my help to get her fully on the other side and that meant putting her to sleep. The next day was such a difficult and sad day for us, but I knew Sophie wasn't going to get better from her cancer and I didn't want to see her in any pain. We loved her too much.

The grief I felt in my heart is taking a long time to heal. I miss her terribly especially at night, because she slept in my arms. There isn't a day that goes by that I don't think about her and my eyes tear up.

I would like to dedicate *My Enlightened Life* in memoriam to Sophie, who was the brightest light in my life, with her star shining bright. I love her with all my heart and she was an important part of our loving family. Just being around her made me feel so happy and content as she purred and purred and then would glance back to look at me and give me those slow closing eyes. I felt her unconditional love go right through me. She had a beautiful star between her eyes and a pure peaceful heart full of love and compassion. She always made me laugh and taught me to be patient with others and to have fun. I always danced and sang songs to her and her brother, Max. Especially, the one that I made up, starting with, "*I love you to the moon and back, yes I do, yes I do, with all my heart...with all of my heart... I love you to the moon and back...*"

When I think about her now, I go deep within my Sacred Heart and feel a sense of joy and gratitude to know Sophie will always be with me. All I have to do is look up at the stars...

Max is still with us and I know he is also grieving her loss. We are around him all the time to show him how much we love and enjoy him in our life.

I know Sophie is happy, free of any pain or discomfort and I know that we will cross each other's path again. I know Sophie will find me and I will find her. Hopefully, one day in the near future. I am attaching a few pictures of Sophie who is black and white, along with a picture of her brother Max who is gray.

One day as I was sitting on the couch with Max, we both heard a meow. He jumped down and I knew it was Sophie letting us know that she was in a happy place. I smiled and I knew that everything was going to be all right.

Dana K. Stone

*D*ana Stone is a highly respected intuitive leader, energy healer and catalyst of change. She harmonizes her vibrational healing skills and knowledge with over 30 years of leadership in California State government, where she catalyzed program and organization culture change.

She is known for her wise counsel, creativity and dedication to helping individuals and groups achieve personal and strategic goals through aligned awareness and the power of joy. Dana intuitively mentors, coaches and inspires her clients to gain absolute clarity on their authentic desires in harmony with their spirit and then rapidly attain success in their lives.

Educated in Europe, she is a University of California alumnus, certified in several vibrational healing and wellness modalities and is a certified graduate of the iPEC (personal empowerment) coaching program. Also passionate about fitness and dance, Dana is a certified Jazzercise instructor in Newcastle California. She and her husband Dennis live nearby in the town of Loomis, California.

Contact Information:

Website: www.danakstone.com
Facebook.com/danakstone

Raise Your Soul's Vibration and Live in Joy

By Dana K. Stone

The surgery has just begun. All preparations have been successful. The terrier's chest has been cracked and is being held wide open. It is now time to test the effect of various chemical solutions on the heart. There are four of us in my surgical student team. The oldest is 25 years old, the youngest is me at 18. It is my turn to be the team lead. I have volunteered for the hardest surgery.

Having demonstrated skilled hands and unflappable logic and calm in prior surgeries, I get what I asked for. As I prep the syringe for the first experiment to record the impact of adrenaline on the heart, out of nowhere I feel a sudden and major rush of anxiety. I immediately push it away. "I can do this," I tell myself. I take a deep breath.

As I extend my hands toward the dog's chest, even before dispensing the contents of the syringe, the dog's heart begins to pulse frantically and out of control. Suddenly, I am jarred out of my hyper-focused attention and my heart starts to pound painfully too. I remove my hands and breathe more deeply, trying to get my own pulse under control.

I hear a voice in my head say, "Okay, no big deal, step back, check the vitals." So I bite my lip and look over to see if the dog's vitals have changed and the anesthesia drip is okay. Nothing is amiss. Nothing has changed. I look down and see the dog's heart is starting to beat more rhythmically.

"Okay," I tell myself, "weird but okay." I begin my silent mantra. "You can do this. You can do this. Everything is a go."

However, when I take another deep breath, suddenly my eyes start to fill with tears. MY HEART REALLY REALLY HURTS. Wait, this should not be happening. I am prepared, I studied hard. I know I can do this. I can't fall apart now. I CAN'T FAIL.

Terrified, I thrust my now-shaking hands again toward the gaping hole in the dog's chest. The dog's heart begins another rapid staccato beat. And all of a sudden, I break into a cold sweat. No thoughts. Just feelings of alternating terror and deep, deep sorrow sweep through me. And there is PAIN, so much pain.

And suddenly, I see myself cowering while being beaten. *Wait! It's not me; is it the dog? How can that be? Why I am feeling her pain?* "Stop feeling, stop feeling," I say over and over to myself. "Think, don't feel. Think, don't feel."

As I try to rein in the cascading emotions, I hear a small, child-like voice whispering, "It's okay. I can take it. I can be better. I can make them love me. I can try harder. I can be what they want. I can be perfect. Really I can."

A blur of scattered thoughts and images begin racing, unbidden, through my mind. I "see" the dog being badly treated by uncaring people. People who cannot see, feel or understand that this poor, defenseless animal just needs to be loved. There is so much love she had to give, tried to give, but it's been rejected over and over. But still she tries. It's in her nature to try, to be loyal, even in the face of cruelty. And she tried so hard.

So many feelings are flooding through me. I can't think. I can't find the calm. I am freaking out. Oh God, I can't breathe. I feel faint. My calm, logical and pragmatic self has abandoned me. I am now starting to panic as my worst fear is being realized. I am about to fail. Big time! And not just some little exam I can make up later, but a full-blown professional humiliation the repercussions of which I cannot even fathom as a pounding headache begins threatening to split my skull in two.

I realize I am going into shock and through the agonizing mist of pain, voices long repressed begin screaming in my head. "You are hopeless. You can't do this. You are weak. You are a failure. You are not good enough. No one loves you."

I close my eyes praying for relief from this internal assault, when suddenly I see and feel the life path and soul of this poor, mistreated dog and hear my own soul reflected in her story and her pain. Her history flashes in images before me. Not knowing why or how, I have merged with the energy field of this poor pound puppy. A mistreated terrier has valiantly given up her life so that pre-med students can learn the intricate workings of a mammalian heart. She has willingly sacrificed her life in service to others. I feel humbled and shaken to my core seeing with physical eyes and for the first time psychic eyes, this vulnerable and exposed heart that in many ways reflects my own.

It feels like a long forever that I am frozen in time, unable to process gut-wrenching feelings and new sensations that have been unleashed from my own heart space and into my conscious awareness. I am floundering and lost in a sea of regret, compassion, blind fear and a seemingly endless well of pain "knowing" some-where deep in my bones that something irrevocable has been unleashed from within.

Finally, my lab partner removes the syringe from my hands. And silently, with tears streaming down my face, I slowly move to the head of the surgical table where I watch the experiments I was to lead, being performed without my assistance. I know somewhere in my heart and deep in my soul, I am about to profoundly disappoint my family and many of my ancestors. I know deep in my bones, I cannot be an MD in the traditional medical model. But what I had yet to know and later discover is that my heightened sensitivities and intuitive attunement would enable me to help others heal at the vibrational level of spirit.

* * * * *

And so began the journey of healing my own heart and the birth of my spirit healing consciousness. I could no longer deny what, deep down inside, I always suspected was true. Not only did I not want to be a doctor, my revelation that I possessed intuitive and even psychic healing abilities rocked me to my core.

Prior to the surgery, I misguidedly tried to fit the family mold. I snuffed out my authentic spark of the joyful me as I tried to "earn love" and live my life by being the "good girl," the responsible one and doing everything but what my heart desired. I let my head rule my heart. I learned to think first and ignore any feelings that came up (or that I sensed and instinctively knew) would not be pleasing to others. I rejected anything that felt unpleasant or painful by just not dealing with it. This was very easy to do as I grew up in an intellectual family where the expectation was the first born would become an MD.

When I was three years old, I went on house calls with my grandfather, who was a physician. Dressed in a nurse's white cap and blue cape, like Florence Nightingale, I wore a stethoscope around my neck and proudly parroted back to my grandfather that "I am not a nurse; I am a doctor." I was even introduced to his patients as "my granddaughter, the MD." The pump was primed and my conditioning reinforced at every turn. There were no other professional options and no other choices. The clear message was do as expected to receive care, love and support. *Go against our wishes and our love will be withdrawn. You will be punished. You will be abandoned. And you will have earned and deserve the pain that ensues.*

At the age of five, my proclamation that I wanted to be a ballet dancer was met with a clear "no way" from the adults around me. I was informed ballet was not my calling or my purpose unless I wanted to starve to death and be on the outs with the founding fathers (meaning my dad, uncle and grandad), who were allopathic medical doctors.

The message to my developing brain was clear. *Do what we want or be abandoned.* I was a "Hayes," an Irish name meaning healer. Even our family crest is a caduceus (the coiled snake around the sword), the medical symbol for healer. And what I had yet to discover was there were other ways to embody my healer heritage.

A "healer" can be more than a traditional medical doctor and healing, (which means to make whole) can take place on more than just the physical level. A vibrational healer addresses more than body mechanics. A vibrational healer helps balance and aligns the individual's entire energy system on the physical, mental, emotional and spiritual level.

However, in my youth, everything was black or white in my head-driven world. At the convent school I attended and university afterwards, I put tons of pressure on myself to get good grades, which meant all A's. I even had to take Royal Academy of Music proficiency exams for the musical instruments I played. There was always so much pressure to perform well and little time for play, fun and enjoyment. The message was clear. Perform well and achieve so you can be loved. So much focus and attention was placed on doing well to validate self-worth, there was little time or value placed on feelings, emotions, and heartfelt desires.

If anything, while growing up, my intuitive and psychic abilities were labeled as "overly sensitive" and I was taught to ignore what I felt and carry on as expected. From this familial messaging, I developed the belief that the real me, the authentic me, was not worthy of existence. Her sole purpose was "to do" and "do brilliantly" whatever was asked and whatever was expected.

So I trained myself to be the smart one. Be the leader. Earn respect and you will not be abandoned. And it was not until my senior year in college (with medical school looming large) that reality set in and the illnesses began. I developed stomach ulcers, which got worse the closer I got to graduation. The pain was almost crippling at times, especially during surgical labs but seemed to ease up on the weekends. However, it was not until the dog heart surgery, I just 'knew" I could not pursue a traditional medical career. I then informed my parents being an allopathic medical doctor was not for me.

Their disappointment was as profound as my realization that I had no idea what to do with the rest of my life. So I began exploring. I knew I genuinely wanted to help others and ultimately be of service.

Following my heart and inner guidance, I spent the next eight years working in the California legislature. Four of those years were spent on getting landmark legislation passed to protect children from child abuse and find permanent homes for hard-to-adopt children. The next 22 years were spent implementing landmark recycling and conservation legislation in California, supervising a multi-million dollar program and budget while raising a family. By anyone's standards, my outer life was a model of success. However, internally, there was an odyssey of physical pain and suffering intertwined with true self-discovery and alignment with my vibrational healing skills.

It took me a while "to get it." As I followed my intellect (what I thought I should be doing and what was expected of me) instead of what I felt was true for me, along with my outer success, I developed a massive infection requiring a hysterectomy at age 30, blew out my adrenals creating severe allergies and auto-immune illness and had part of my colon removed followed by six long years of chronic back pain. This is what can happen when your spirit, the "true you energy" is denied, ignored and not allowed to flow. A stagnant spirit creates a low energy vibration which then becomes the breeding ground for toxins and disease.

While many would consider any one of the above maladies completely debilitating, to me, from my intellectual perspective, they were mere inconveniences. I processed illness solely through my body and my mind and completely ignored the feelings that had triggered and created them. With each illness, some part of me always knew that I would be okay. I would overcome. I would survive. I would learn and grow.

With each illness, I was literally stopped in my tracks and since I could not distract myself with "doing," I had to learn to just "be." And just "being" was where the emotions and feelings came up, the inner reflections deepened and true healing occurred. It was from the seat of illness that I began to learn, explore and expand my inner awareness, intuition and connection with my soul's consciousness.

When I determined the "why" of an illness, the how to correct the imbalance came easily to me. And interestingly, it led to the development and acceptance of my spirit healing gifts and the desire to share them with others.

When I learned I had a gift for traveling energy pathways of non-ordinary reality and super consciousness, my energy soared. I conducted and practiced vibrational healing first for myself and then for others. And it is through these experiences, embracing all levels of body, mind and spirit, that I systematized a process for clearing energy blocks, past, present and future using my clairvoyant, clairaudient and clairsentient skills to raise my energy and vibration.

After my epic fail in the surgery lab, I had (and continue to have) lucid and psychic dreams. My favorite is the one in which I watched my essence (like a white cirrus cloud) leave my body and float by the mirror in my home. I also began to consciously acknowledge and practice my intuitive gifts, not only doing astrology and tarot readings for friends and colleagues, but dream interpretations as well. While working to protect "nature" and the environment (through the energy of recycling and reusing the old to create the new), I also explored energy and vibrational healing in as many forms and ways as possible. I did energy scans and readings for work colleagues and brought healing crystals to contentious meetings at work.

I discovered I loved traveling through the Southwest, learning more and more about the spiritual and healing practices of my ancestors. I studied shamanic practices in an apprenticeship program to learn the healing energy of plants, crystals and animals. And with each of my own physical challenges (from migraines and mysterious skin rashes to a twisted colon), I learned to access joyful and creative parts of myself long forgotten or blocked and in need of healing. I was healing my spirit through my life experience and found joy in teaching others how to do the same.

That day in the lab, when the dog's heart responded to the vibration of my hands and I accepted as real my first "conscious psychic wash" and my ability to "read" energy simply by "being me," I opened the doorway to accept my true purpose as a vibrational healer and catalyst of change. Learning to follow my intuition and internal wisdom thereafter, which many times seemed diametrically opposed to my "logical mind and intellect," I discovered that intention and acceptance of my true nature were the keys to becoming whole.

When I "laser-focused" on learning the "energy of the lesson" (listening and then acting on my intuition and using my divine gifts), I stopped repeating old habits and patterns out of lack of awareness and fear. When I was intuitively able to (1) identify the core problem, (2) clear limiting beliefs and release old patterns of thinking, (3) embrace inner knowing and (4) follow inner guidance and wisdom, wellness was always the result. Deep within, I had been raised and trained to believe that everything can be healed. And while sometimes the healing is the acceptance of the condition itself, sometimes the cure is through spiritual or non-traditional ways of handling the imbalance to restore the wellness.

What I have also come to realize is that as I express more and more of who I really know myself to be, a catalyst of love and joy, my health has been the best ever. I learned that I am a highly sensitive empath responsible for maintaining the integrity of my own energy boundaries, which, without awareness, can too easily blend with others, upsetting my own natural balance. I learned that when I ignore or cut off my creativity, pain manifests immediately. I have learned that with awareness of my thoughts and following the whisperings of my heart (which is not madness, as I previously had been led to believe) my inner wisdom guides me to express more and more of who I am and who I want to be.

I believe it is crucial for each person to acknowledge their true loving nature and allow their dreams to be fulfilled. Joy is love to the infinite power. And when we align our gratitude (for all we have), intention, and conscious awareness with true self-knowledge, we experience joy.

When we listen to and act upon our inner wisdom, the Universe through the law of attraction powerfully supports us (often in miraculous ways). When we consciously and consistently shift into positive modes of thinking and act as guided by our intuition, we grow our unique talents and abilities, raise our soul's vibration and manifest the life of our dreams.

It is not hard to move in harmony with the energies of the Universe and the life force that energizes and ignites spiritual growth and evolution. It can be accomplished with joyful practice and joyful learning. I have the gift of shining the light for others on their path of joy. I then teach them how to detect, reflect and connect with joy consistently to sustain their joy momentum.

When we are aligned with our spirit, we feed our heart and fuel our soul. It is my privilege and purpose to help others align with their true joy. Whether working with individuals or groups, in live and virtual events, my focus is on helping individuals shift their consciousness from a pain dynamic to a pleasure principle and address any imbalances in their energetic system(s).

I enjoy being a global speaker, sharing information and demonstrating tools, tips and techniques on how to "raise the soul's vibration through the art of living in joy." And my classes, workshops, individual and group coaching are designed to help each person raise their vibration and reach their highest and best potential while leading a joy-filled life. Sometimes called the "Joy Detective," I love to lead and inspire people to maximize their body-mind-spirit fitness and unleash their power of joy.

Afterword

This book series—*The Inner Circle Chronicles*—has been a blessing to myself and so many. It is unique and transformative in a time in history when illumination and enlightenment and trailblazing mean taking a journey of courage and heart.

Stay tuned for Book 5, in which you will meet women who have broken through glass ceilings, created visionary businesses and continue to advance humanity for the highest good of all concerned.

Thank you for being a part of my journey.

Many blessings,

Anne Deidre

About Inner Visions Publishing

*I*ntuitive Life Coach, best-selling author, and spiritual thought leader Anne Deidre created Inner Vision Publishing in 2013 to offer an avenue for spiritually based authors to share their wisdom with the world. Anne is the editor of collaborative works, in which co-authors contribute a chapter on a particular theme. She also supports individual authors seeking personalized attention, coaching, and intuitive guidance in developing, writing, and publishing their books. In some cases, Anne also helps her clients create and build businesses around their books through workshops, coaching, public speaking, and other modalities.

For more information, please contact:

www.annedeidre.com

ANNE DEIDRE
Inner Visions Publishing
GIVING VOICE TO SPIRITUAL, INTUITIVE
ARTISTS AND WRITERS

CPSIA information can be obtained
at www.ICGtesting.com
Printed in the USA
FFOW01n0014040217
31985FF